GLASS
HOUSES

GLASS
HOUSES

Edited by Alejandro Bahamón

COLLINS|DESIGN
An Imprint of HarperCollinsPublishers

GLASS HOUSES
Copyright © 2006 by COLLINS DESIGN and LOFT Publications

HarperCollins books may be purchased for educational, business, or sales promotional use.
For information, please write: Special Markets Department, HarperCollins Publishers Inc.,
10 East 53rd Street, New York, NY 10022

First Edition published in 2006 by:
Collins Design
An Imprint of HarperCollins*Publishers*
10 East 53rd Street
New York, NY 10022
Tel.: (212) 207-7000
Fax: (212) 207-7654
collinsdesign@harpercollins.com
www.harpercollins.com

Distributed throughout the world by:
HarperCollins*Publishers*
10 East 53rd Street
New York, NY 10022
Fax: (212) 207-7654

Packaged by
LOFT Publications
Via Laietana, 32 4.º Of. 92
08003 Barcelona, Spain
Tel.: +34 932 688 088
Fax: +34 932 687 073
loft@loftpublications.com
www.loftpublications.com

Editor:
Alejandro Bahamón

Translation:
Jay Noden

Art Director:
Mireia Casanovas Soley

Layout:
Zahira Rodríguez Mediavilla

Library of Congress Cataloging-in-Publication Data
Bahamón, Alejandro.
  Glass houses / Alejandro Bahamon.– 1st ed.
    p. cm.
  ISBN-13: 978-0-06-089339-2 (hardcover)
  ISBN-10: 0-06-089339-7 (hardcover)
  1. Glass construction. 2. Architecture, Domestic. I. Title.
  NA7186.B34 2006
  721'.04496–dc22
                        2006007598

Printed in Spain

First Printing, 2006

Table of Contents

Photos: © Jordi Sarrà

Introduction:The evolution of glass house

Industrial revolution

Creating a glass house is one of the most significant design exercises in the evolution of the modern movement. The formal, structural, and constructive implications of a project for a house almost entirely clad in glass exposes the vision of many architects regarding how to live in and construct houses following the industrial revolution. The constructive possibilities that the evolution of techniques and materials presented at the beginning of the 20th century, such as the use of steel, reinforced concrete, and glass are reflected in the architectural proposals from that era. Some non-residential buildings from the end of the 19th century and the beginning of the 20th were precursors to how architects would exploit the qualities of glass: the great Waucquez department stores of Victor Horta; the library at Glasgow's School of Art, famously projected by Charles Renie Mackintosh; the rear façade of the Looshaus in Vienna, by Adolf Loos; and the Glass Pavilion of Bruno Taut. Other buildings moved away from the large-scale constructions of pavilions, such as the famous Crystal Palace, to approach constructions of smaller proportions.

The Maison de Verre, designed in 1928 and built in Paris in 1932, undoubtedly constitutes the great leap in housing architecture, in terms of adapting new technology and incorporating steel and glass into design and construction. Designed by the French architect Pierre Chareau (Bordeaux, France, 1883–New York, United States, 1950), this building, according to the architect himself, was made by craftsmen and its main aim was to standardize. The apartment, made for a married couple, the Dalsaces, forms part of a building, situated in the center of a typical Parisian block. The new project had to respect the building's existing structure, maintain the neighbors' privacy, house a modern gynecologists clinic on the ground floor, and transform the upper floors into a home. The most striking aspect was the front façade, where the original brickwork was entirely replaced by a structure of steel and glass blocks. Chareau created an apartment, which begins with the soft light of the entrance, leads through a well-lit ground floor, before arriving at the shaft belonging to the three floors where the stairs are found. This building is undoubtedly a key construction from the interwar avant-garde, and is halfway between art deco and the aesthetics found in the machine era.

Photos: © Nelson Kon

Latin American experience

Perhaps we would consider a glass house to be a design exercise that requires natural surroundings, more or less protected from any immediate neighbors, to which the interior of the house is opened up. However it requires great sensitivity to detect the subtle characteristics an environment presents and sharp rationality to use those characteristics to create a perfectly integrated project. A clear example of this can be seen in projects from the mid-20th-century in Latin America; fertile ground during the expansion of ideas from the modern movement, for a large amount of conceptual and technical experimentation in architecture. Many European and local architects applied the principles of functional and formal rationalism to their projects, some more successful than others regarding the projects' integration with their environments. South America's lush environment required a careful interpretation, both of its qualities, and of the relationship established between the local inhabitants and their natural surroundings. It would appear that through his contact with the nature there, Lina Bo Bardi (Rome, Italy, 1914–São Paulo, Brazil, 1992) who had lived and worked in South America, became one of the few modern figures to really understand these relations.

The Glass House (São Paulo, 1951) was Lina Bo's first project, after she had immigrated to Brazil and married the well-known journalist and art curator, Pietro Bardi. It constitutes a highly significant development in the construction of this type of house in Latin America. Influences of European architects such as Terragni, Nervi and Le Corbusier can be clearly seen reflected in the design of this house. However, far from merely repeating the models of these masters, Lina Bo Bardi created an original composition, which adapts to Brazil's environment. The house takes us on a thorough and sensual journey, which starts at the access to the plot and develops throughout the interior spaces. It was designed as a private residence for the Bardis themselves, and consists of two bodies, one closed and built directly on the land, and the other open and raised on piles measuring 5 inches in diameter. The first, built from stone, houses the more intimate rooms of the house, and the second, defined by the glass cladding, contains the social area. While the first, closed, draws on traditional construction techniques of the region, the glass body seems to float above the land and connects directly with the garden and the distant views. The interaction between these two volumes creates a unique architectural piece, a symbiosis between the vernacular and the modern avant-garde.

Modern movement

The full possibilities of glass in modern architecture were brought to light by Mies van der Rohe (1886–1969). His theoretical and architectural legacy continues to be an important reference in contemporary architecture regarding structural clarity; a technology applied to architecture and formal refinement. From when he began as an architect in inter-war Germany, Mies van der Rohe showed a keen interest in new technologies, above all in the usage of reinforced concrete, steel frameworks, and glass cladding. The latter was the main subject of his work, and he developed various projects that included covering large surfaces of buildings in glass. A well-known example of his work was the glass skyscraper he designed in 1922, in which already avant-garde concepts were used as the backing structure of glass cladding and a modulated façade, a technique which was to be well developed in this construction.

Farnsworth House (Plano, Illinois, 1951), situated on the banks of the Fox River and some 40 miles to the west of Chicago, constitutes one of Mies van der Rohe's most significant constructions. This was his first open-plan building, which convincingly paved a new way to understanding the modern home. The entire architectural repertoire of traditional houses composed of bedrooms, walls, doors, moldings, furniture, paintings and even personal objects is completely abandoned in favor of a house's simplicity and purity. The building is organized around two horizontal plans, situated above the ground, which form the floor and the roof of the construction. They are supported by peripherally arranged steel beams. This organization allows the interior and the façade to be completely freed of any structural element, creating a completely open-plan interior space, which opens, in its entirety, to the outside via glass cladding. The importance of Farnsworth House, whose design dates back to 1945, was recognized even before its construction. The project was presented in 1947 and a scale model was exhibited in New York's Museum of Modern Art, where the project was considered to be the beginning of a radical proposal in residential architecture. The architecture of this house represents a refinement of Mies van der Rohe's minimalist expression regarding structure and space.

Photos: © Michael Moran

International style

What started as experimental avant-garde projects became more common from the 1950s onward. The architect, Philip Johnson (1906–2005) is a highly significant figure, not only for his construction, but also for other activities he was involved in throughout his professional career. He studied the history of architecture at Harvard University and was director of the recently created department of architecture at New York's Museum of Modern Art. He was critic, author, historian, and museologist, until, at the age of 36, he focused on architecture and designed his first building. He is largely responsible for spreading ideas of the International Style, an architectural movement that was originally formed to adapt the ideas of the Bauhaus to the American environment. No material symbolizes this architectural style better than glass. Philip Johnson took Farnsworth House, designed by his colleague and friend Mies van der Rohe, as a clear reference for designing his Glass House (New Canaan, Connecticut, 1951); it was also know as the Johnson House as it was his private residence. In contrast to Farnsworth House, it is symmetrical and sits firmly on the ground. Low furnishings and a brick cylinder, which contains the bathroom, divide the inside. The building is entirely covered in glass and the metal structure is of a minimum thickness, thereby making the house completely transparent in its natural surroundings.

Le Corbusier, father of modern architecture, declared in the 1920s that the history of architecture was the history of the conquest of the window. This statement has become a fundamental principle of contemporary architecture. Today's architects, instead of considering the window as a mere opening in the wall, which allows light and air to enter, see glass as a space-defining material. In turn, manufacturers of glass for architecture have improved its qualities regarding visibility, insulation, safety, and comfort. Today covering a building in glass has become a sophisticated system that solves problems of lighting, ventilation, humidity, dust, noise, climate control, and even protection from ultraviolet and infrared rays. The following pages are a summary of today's most innovative proposals of the use of glass in architecture: as the building's structural element—in Laminata House, by Kruunenberg van der Erve Architecten; as the material used for an exterior finish without taking advantage of its transparency; in Nigg House, by Graser Architekten; or making the most of its energy saving possibilities, like in SolarTube House, by Driendl Architects. The depth with which each of these is analysed, via detailed plans, allows the reader to clearly see what these types of houses can achieve almost a century after the first proposals of the modern avant-gardists came to light.

The natural slope of the plot and the house's development on a single story mean that the front section has to be suspended on piles, in order to raise it about 2 meters above the ground. This emphasizes the lightness of the glass façade and is used to store gardening equipment.

CASA T

Architect: **FEYFERLIK / FRITZER**

Location: GRAZ, AUSTRIA

Date of construction: 2005

Photography: © ANGELO KAUNAT

The plot where this house is built slopes gently towards the southeast and forms part of a former garden, with lush vegetation of large and medium-sized trees as well as great views over the nearby valley. The fundamental premise when designing this house was therefore to take advantage of these great trees, and to be able to enjoy the surroundings from the inside and various other points. Due to these delicate surroundings, a single-story construction was chosen, which blends with the trees and minimizes the visual impact on the environment.

The house is organized on a longitudinal plan, which develops parallel to the curves of the plot and faces the views. The east, south, and west façades consist of a continuous layer of glass, which folds around capturing the best possible panoramas of the landscape from all rooms of the house. The 73-foot long interior is entirely void of columns due to a metal beam visible on the ceiling, emphasizing the visual permeability and the connection with the exterior. The north façade is covered in a black membrane, in order to best camouflage the most solid part of the house.

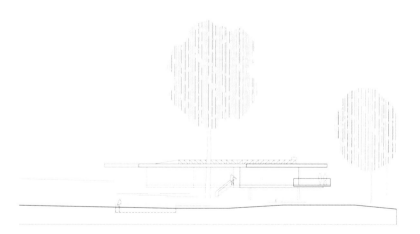

The angled geometry of the plan corresponds as much to the topography as to the position of the trees. In order to avoid felling any of these trees, the perimeter of the house has been adjusted to their random positions. One has even been incorporated into the body of the house.

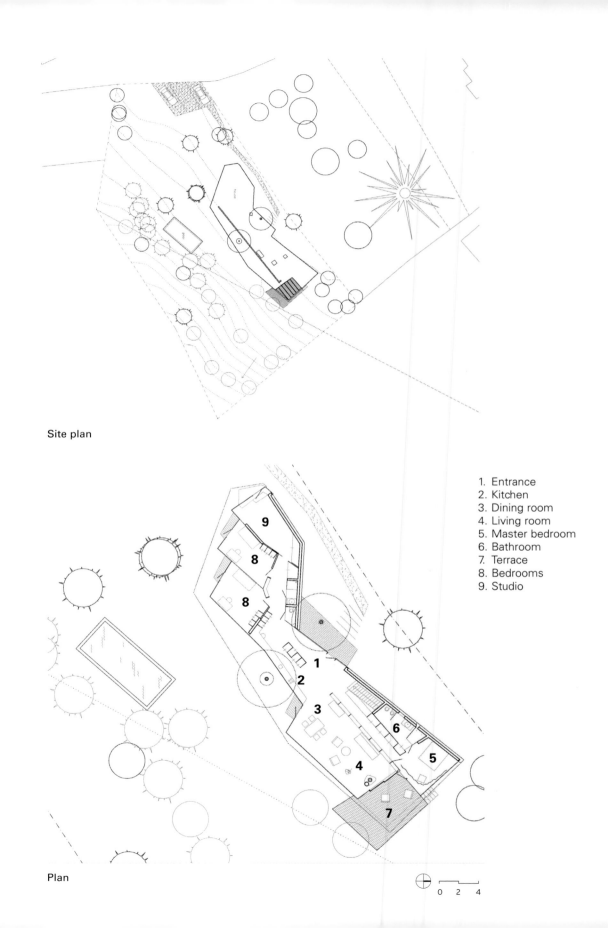

Site plan

1. Entrance
2. Kitchen
3. Dining room
4. Living room
5. Master bedroom
6. Bathroom
7. Terrace
8. Bedrooms
9. Studio

Plan

0 2 4

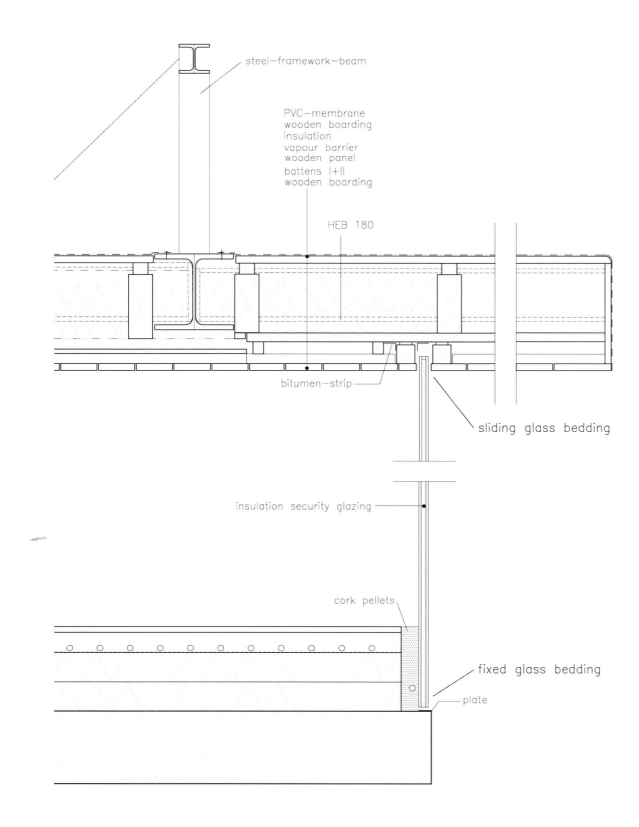

steel—framework—beam

PVC—membrane
wooden boarding
insulation
vapour barrier
wooden panel
battens I+II
wooden boarding

HEB 180

bitumen—strip

sliding glass bedding

insulation security glazing

cork pellets

fixed glass bedding

plate

The large windows in this house are completely embedded in the roof framework, in the slots where the aluminum beams are inserted. The metal supports have been hidden on the lower section by positioning them below the floor of the ground floor.

Construction details

The glass that covers the rooms of the house and the black ceramic, which covers the closed façade, attempt to reflect the surroundings and in doing so integrate the building with the environment.

8 X 8 HOUSE

Architect: **FELIPE ASSADI**

Location: CALERA DE TANGO, CHILE

Date of construction: 2005

Photography: © GUY WENBORNE

The design of this house began with an 8 inch x 8 inch ceramic piece. The measurements of this decorative box have been used to design its structure and decorations right down to the smallest details and the furniture inside. The construction has a square 36 feet x 36 feet plan with an outside height of 11.3 feet, and was conceived as a glass box, which is closed only on one side. The commission was to create a guest house, with two en suite bedrooms and a games room, within a flat landscape, protected by a thick layer of trees that surrounds it. As well as the self-imposed restriction on the regulating module, the house could not exceed 1076 square feet.

The house developed from a ceramic box, within which a predominantly transparent volume was inserted. Due to the lack of space, the kitchen, bar, and guests bathroom, were organized into a single section within the space, which also separates the bedrooms from the living room. The dining room was moved out to the terrace, an exterior space yet contained within the box, to form a fitted piece of furniture, which also adapts to the module.

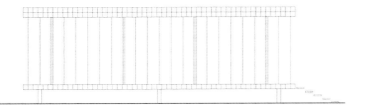

The closed west-facing wall
has a barbecue on the inside
face, a small kitchen, and
a space for the gas bottles.
A table and a long bench
was also built into the
space covered in 0.8 x 0.8
in ceramic tiles.

1. Entrance
2. Dining room
3. Family room
4. Kitchen
5. Bathroom
6. Bedrooms
7. Bathrooms

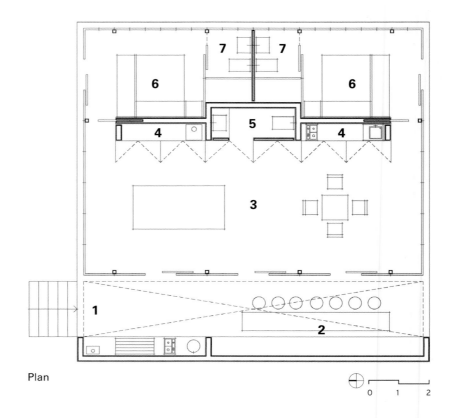

Plan

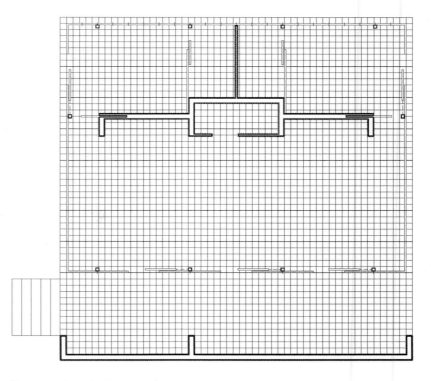

Pavement layout plan

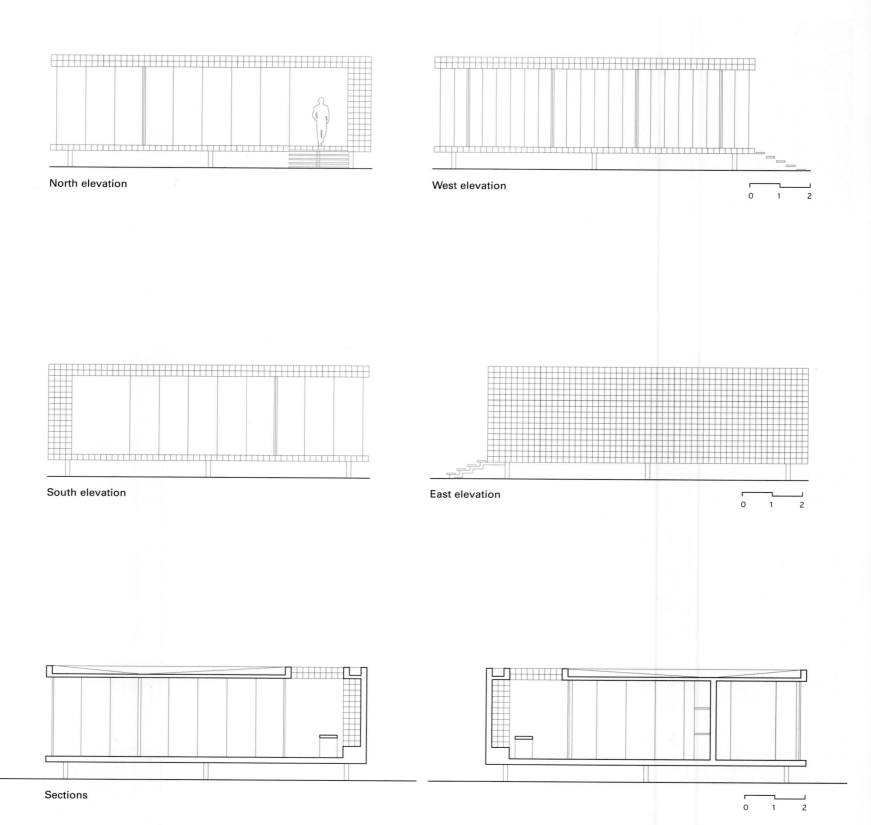

North elevation

West elevation

0   1   2

South elevation

East elevation

0   1   2

Sections

0   1   2

The application of modern technology and materials, such as insulating glass, the covering of vegetation, or the mechanic ventilation, was one of the design premises. The structure of metal beams is reinforced with steel cables, which give the building rigidity.

DENIS HOUSE

Architects: **DETHIER & ASSOCIÉS**

Collaborators: JEAN GLIBERT (ARTIST), LAURENT NEY (STRUCTURE)

Location: JEHANSTER-VERVIERS, BELGIUM

Date of construction: 2000

Photography: © JEAN PAUL LEGROS

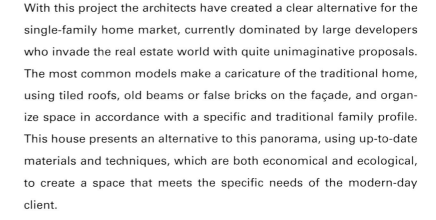

With this project the architects have created a clear alternative for the single-family home market, currently dominated by large developers who invade the real estate world with quite unimaginative proposals. The most common models make a caricature of the traditional home, using tiled roofs, old beams or false bricks on the façade, and organize space in accordance with a specific and traditional family profile. This house presents an alternative to this panorama, using up-to-date materials and techniques, which are both economical and ecological, to create a space that meets the specific needs of the modern-day client.

This building is designed around an entirely prefabricated, light box, which rises from concrete foundations in the middle of an orchard in Jehanster, some 8 miles from Verviers, in Belgium. The metal structure and the transparent and opaque glass covering generate a total symbiosis with its environment and offers its occupants an intimate connection with their natural surroundings. A grapevine entwines itself around the cables that hold the south façade secure, creating a natural climate control system, and at the same time connecting it to the surroundings. The shadows from the leaves form an insulation chamber in front of the façade and protect the interior from overheating in the summer.

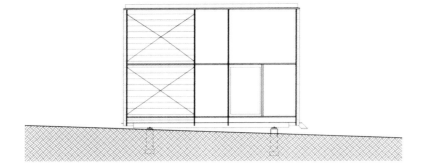

The structure of the metal pillar parameter, which supports a light roof of the same material, allows for a free plan, which can be distributed depending on the user's needs. A mid-height volume was created inside, in the middle of the space, which contains the bathroom and the main bedroom, on top of which is a study.

Ground floor

1. Entrance
2. Living room
3. Dining - kitchen
4. Library
5. Master bedroom
6. Bathroom
7. Laundry
8. Parking

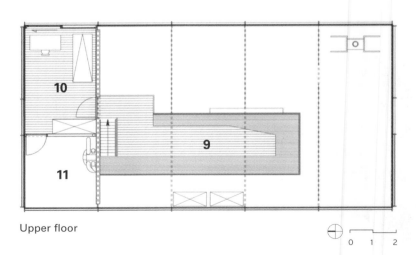

Upper floor

9. Studio
10. Bedroom
11. Cellar

0   1   2

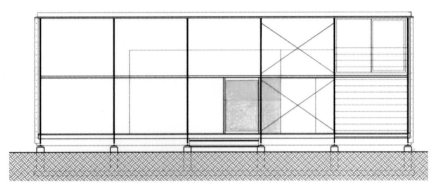

East elevation

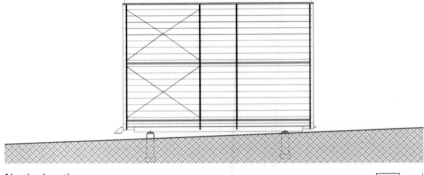

North elevation

0   1   2

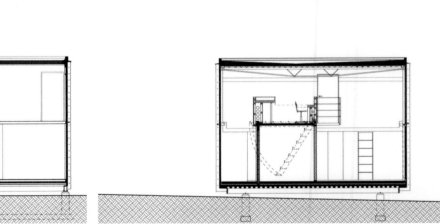

Longitudinal section

Transversal section

0   1   2

The framework of the floor and roof has been made using metal sheets filled with a fine layer of concrete. This system allows the sheets to distribute the weight, gives shape to the framework using small joists and considerably reduces its depth.

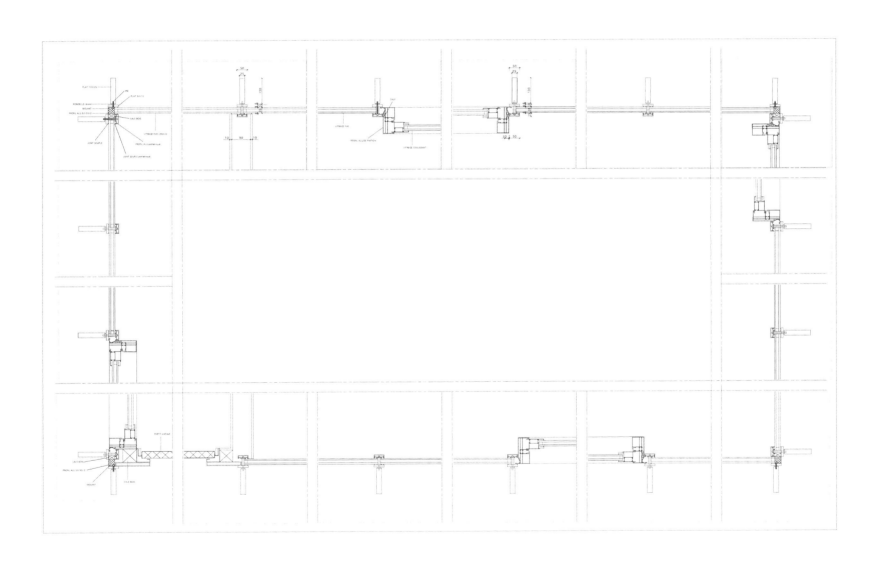

Construction details

On the concrete base stands a light metal structure composed of the bedroom and terrace. A walkway on piles, which blend with the tree trunks, enters the forest like an observatory. The plantation of bamboo trees alongside the walkway reinforces this effect.

MOUNTAIN GUEST HOUSE

Architects: **MACK SCOGIN MERRILL ELAM ARCHITECTS**

Location: DILLARD, GA, USA

Date of construction: 2001

Photography: ©TIMOTHY HURSLEY

This construction constitutes the second phase of a project for a home, started more than five years ago. The original house, just a few feet from this one, consists of a building which is closely related to the exterior, using patios, terraces, and large glass surfaces, designed as a second home to enjoy the tranquility of this lush forest. With the passing of time and as the family grew it became necessary to enlarge the project to create more space for guests, as well as for tractors, and dogs. The new building consists of a garage, a guest room with bathroom, and a large bamboo terrace.

The design was meant to be an enlargement of the original house, not only functionally but also formally. In this sense it was created as a space that diminishes the borders between outside and in, upper and lower, heavy and light. From one side of the house a room can be seen inside a glass box that seems to be suspended in the air; from the other side, there is a walkway that leads into the forest. A structure of reinforced concrete that houses the garage and the storeroom acts as a base for the rest of the building, which is built from metal and glass.

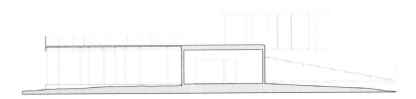

The privileged location of the house, in the south of the Appalachian Mountain range in the United States, has been the major factor in the design of the project. The 24.25-acre plot's greatest feature is the dense forest of slender poplars that covers it, generating an atmosphere of privacy and seclusion.

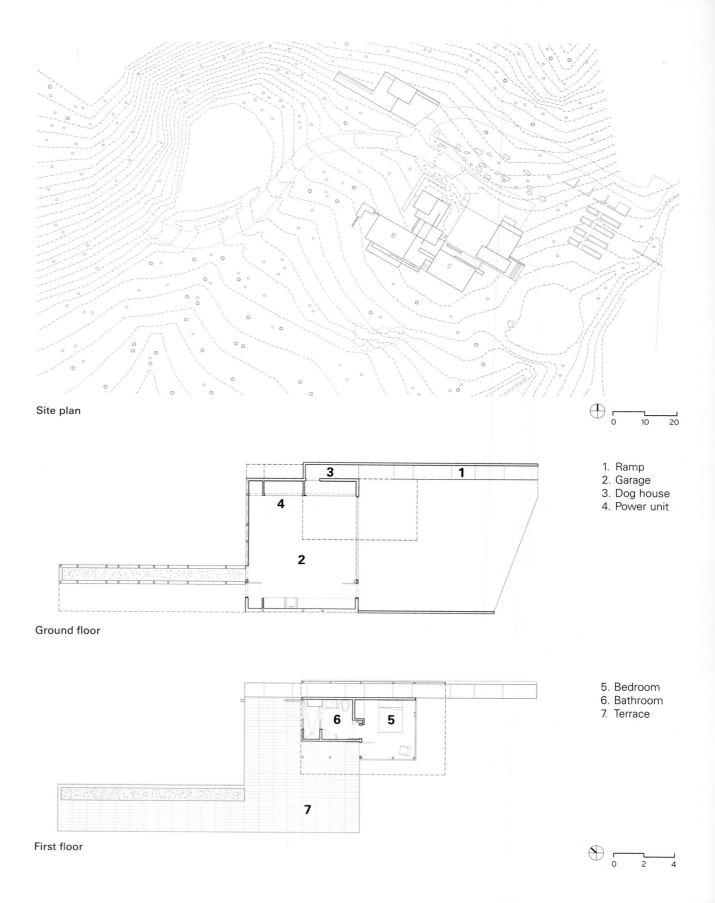

Site plan

0   10   20

Ground floor

1. Ramp
2. Garage
3. Dog house
4. Power unit

First floor

5. Bedroom
6. Bathroom
7. Terrace

0   2   4

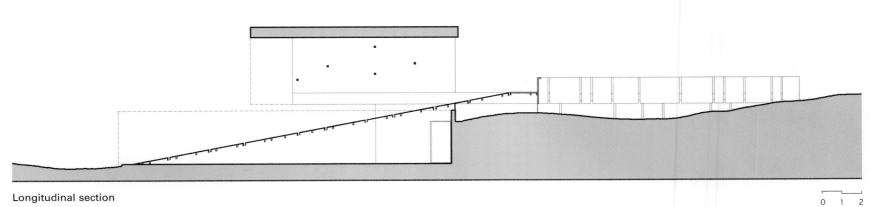

Longitudinal section

0 1 2

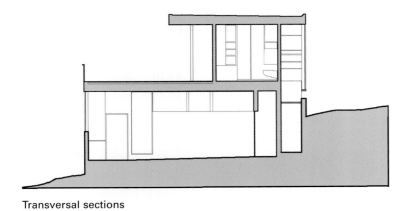

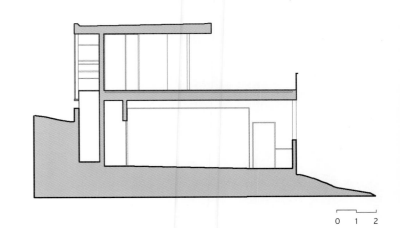

Transversal sections

0 1 2

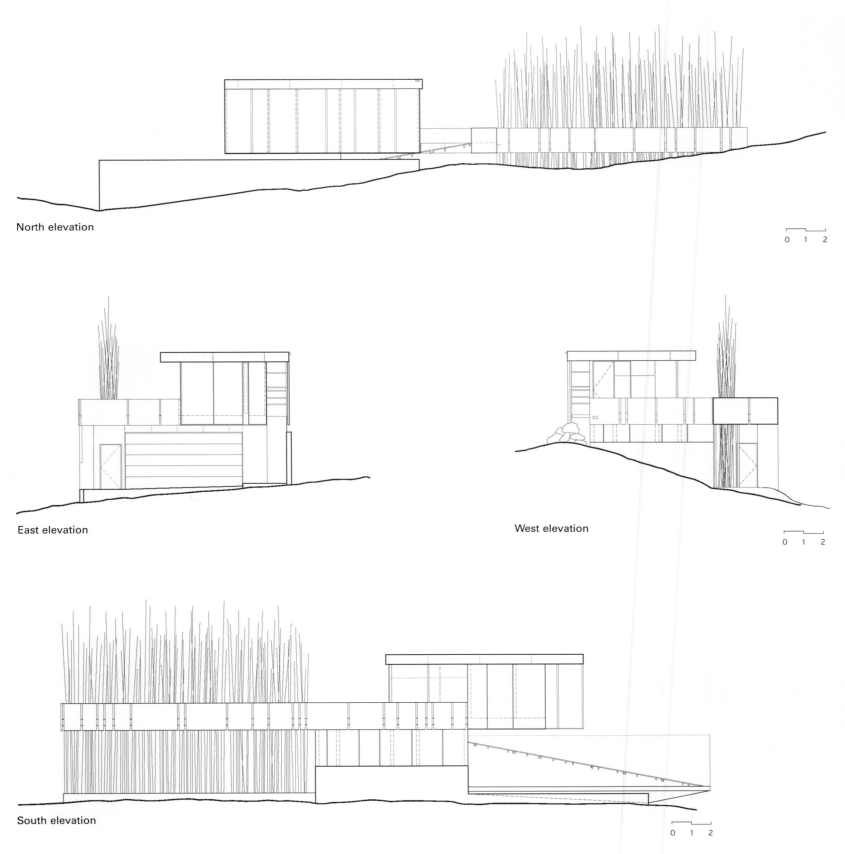

North elevation

0 1 2

East elevation

West elevation

0 1 2

South elevation

0 1 2

The metal frames that support the windows are set into the upper framework to bring the glass right up to the ceiling. This detail minimizes the visible width of the window frames and emphasizes the transparency of the volume.

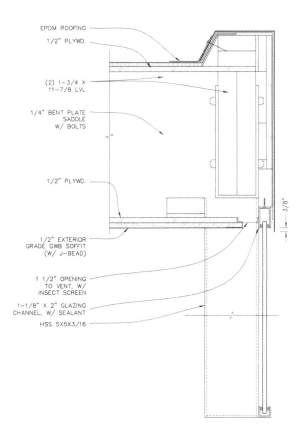

EPDM ROOFING
1/2" PLYWD.

(2) 1-3/4 X 11-7/8 LVL

1/4" BENT PLATE SADDLE W/ BOLTS

1/2" PLYWD.

1/2" EXTERIOR GRADE GWB SOFFIT (W/ J-BEAD)

1 1/2" OPENING TO VENT, W/ INSECT SCREEN

1-1/8" X 2" GLAZING CHANNEL, W/ SEALANT

HSS 5X5X3/16

3/8"

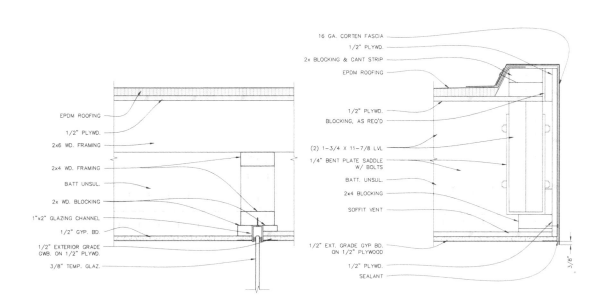

EPDM ROOFING
1/2" PLYWD.
2x6 WD. FRAMING

2x4 WD. FRAMING

BATT UNSUL.

2x WD. BLOCKING

1"x2" GLAZING CHANNEL

1/2" GYP. BD.

1/2" EXTERIOR GRADE GWB. ON 1/2" PLYWD.

3/8" TEMP. GLAZ.

16 GA. CORTEN FASCIA
1/2" PLYWD.
2x BLOCKING & CANT STRIP
EPDM ROOFING

1/2" PLYWD.
BLOCKING, AS REQ'D

(2) 1-3/4 X 11-7/8 LVL
1/4" BENT PLATE SADDLE W/ BOLTS
BATT. UNSUL.
2x4 BLOCKING

SOFFIT VENT

1/2" EXT. GRADE GYP BD. ON 1/2" PLYWOOD
1/2" PLYWD.
SEALANT

3/8"

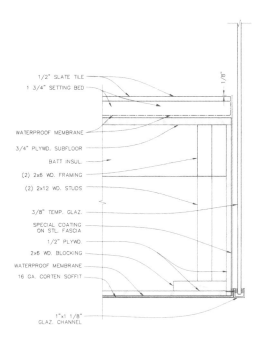

1/2" SLATE TILE
1 3/4" SETTING BED

1/8"

WATERPROOF MEMBRANE
3/4" PLYWD. SUBFLOOR
BATT INSUL.
(2) 2x6 WD. FRAMING
(2) 2x12 WD. STUDS

3/8" TEMP. GLAZ.
SPECIAL COATING ON STL. FASCIA
1/2" PLYWD.
2x6 WD. BLOCKING
WATERPROOF MEMBRANE
16 GA. CORTEN SOFFIT

1"x1 1/8" GLAZ. CHANNEL

Construction details

The protruding roof and floor slabs protect the interior from the sun. These slabs incorporate a system of natural ventilation, which helps to cool the inside of the house during the hottest months of the year.

BUTTERFLY HOUSE

Architect: **LIPPMANN ASSOCIATES**

Location: SYDNEY, AUSTRALIA

Date of construction: 2005

Photography: © WILLEM RETHMEIER

The house is located on the rocky coastline of Dover Heights, in Sydney, Australia and offers splendid views of the Pacific Ocean toward the east and of Sydney Bay and the financial district toward the west. The client, a Malaysian property developer, wanted this house to accommodate his family and set two determining guidelines. The building was to avoid any straight lines and the design had to incorporate Feng Shui principles, the Chinese science of architecture and space. The composition of the building is based on these premises and consists of two separate and interdependent wings. The east wing receives the morning sun and houses the bedrooms, and the west wing basks in the sunsets and splendid views of the bay and houses the living area. A basement is used as a large garage and a cinema.

The building's structure as well as the massive use of glass and light aluminum profiles gives the composition the appearance of a sculpture. A mesh of metal columns supports the concrete slabs, which protrude to create balconies and a wide protection from the sun. The terrace at the east end of the house offers an 180° panoramic view over the ocean, the nearby cliffs, Sydney Bay, the Harbor Bridge, and the Opera House.

Just as the general
volumetric plan is divided
into east and west wings,
the project uses the two
floors to differentiate the
living area and the children's
area on the ground floor
from the parents' more
private area on the first floor.

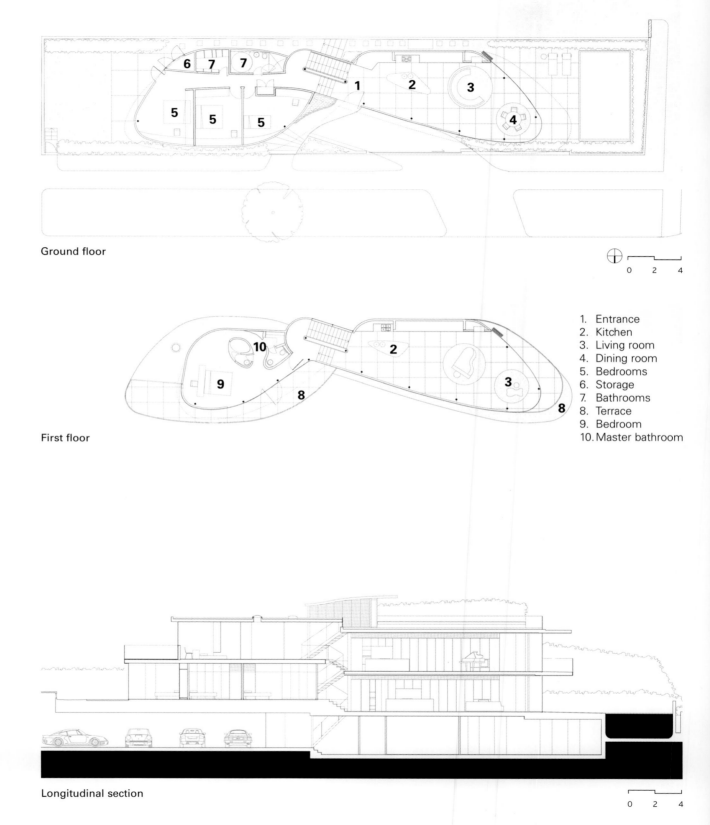

Ground floor

First floor

1. Entrance
2. Kitchen
3. Living room
4. Dining room
5. Bedrooms
6. Storage
7. Bathrooms
8. Terrace
9. Bedroom
10. Master bathroom

Longitudinal section

The edges of the slabs have been finished with strips of aluminum. On the outdoor terraces, this helps to hide the angles that support the curved glass of the railings.

Construction details

The materials and finishes of the house were chosen based on their integration with the landscape. The metal frames that support the house, as well as the railings made from the same material, were left to oxidize, producing a patinated effect. The terraces are formed by a galvanized grating, which allows the water to pass.

VILLA LUCY

Architects: **WPA**

Location: PORT TOWNSEND, WA, USA

Date of construction: 2004

Photography: © LARA SWIMMER, PHILIP NEWTON

This weekend home is situated in idyllic surroundings, on a hillside, surrounded by a thick pine forest, and looking out over the Juan de Fuca strait in Washington. The architects, also the owners of the house, saw the house's integration with the landscape and local ecosystem as their fundamental premise. For this reason an elevated platform was created that appears to float above the land and allows the vegetation and rain to run freely beneath the house. Six steel frames, made in the workshop to avoid damaging the plot's vegetation, support the platform.

The composition develops around two longitudinal bodies, which run parallel to the slope of the site. The first volume, which is closed and covered in wood, accommodates the amenities such as the kitchen, bathroom and storage. A second body, which is totally open to the surroundings and covered in glass, houses the living rooms, dining room, and bedrooms. The latter has an exterior space in the form of a patio, also open to the views. The entrance is a metal bridge behind the wooden volume standing out against the forest backdrop as it enters the house.

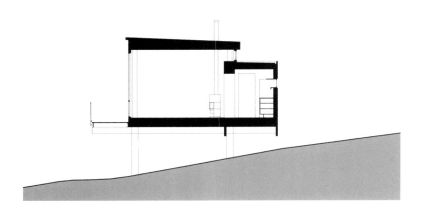

The transparent body of the
house is composed of three
materials: wood, which
carries out a structural role,
aluminum, as insulating
frames for the windows, and
glass, which gives the
transparency to the outside.

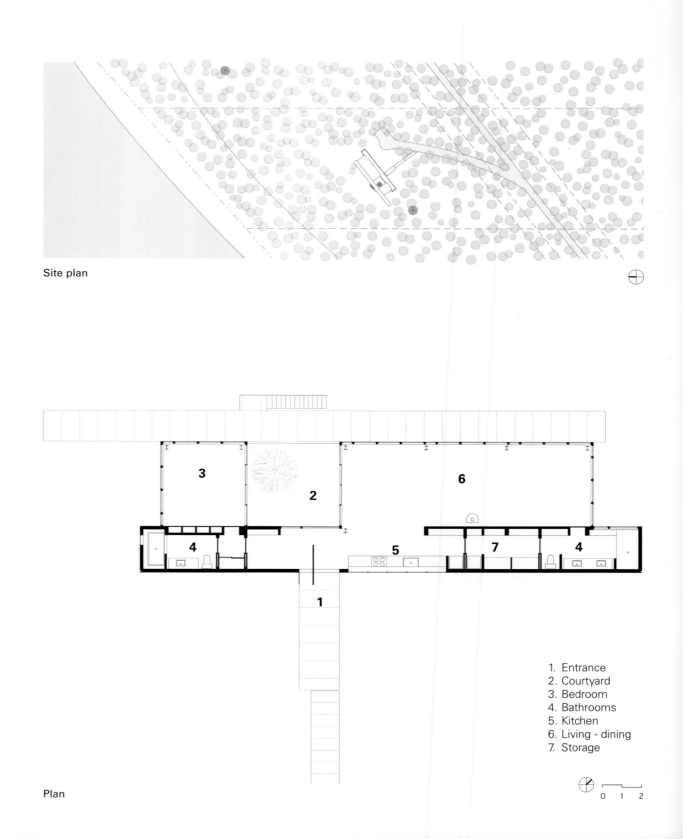

Site plan

Plan

1. Entrance
2. Courtyard
3. Bedroom
4. Bathrooms
5. Kitchen
6. Living - dining
7. Storage

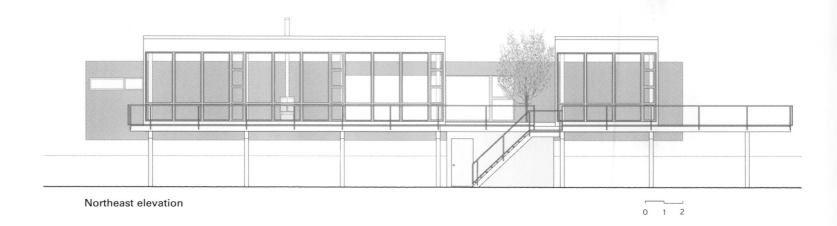

Northeast elevation

0 1 2

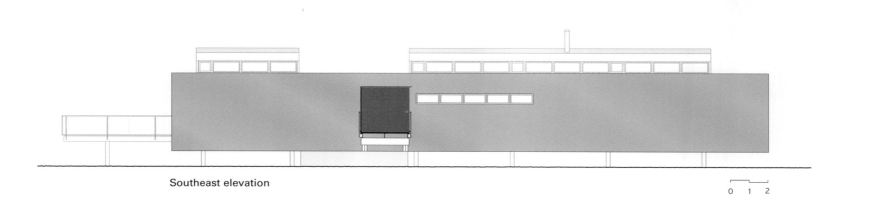

Southeast elevation

0 1 2

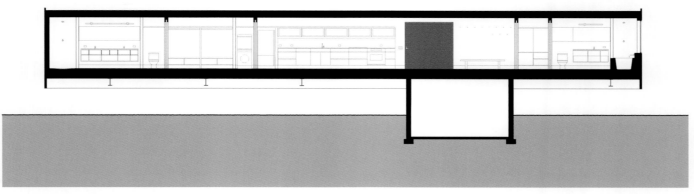

Longitudinal section

0 1 2

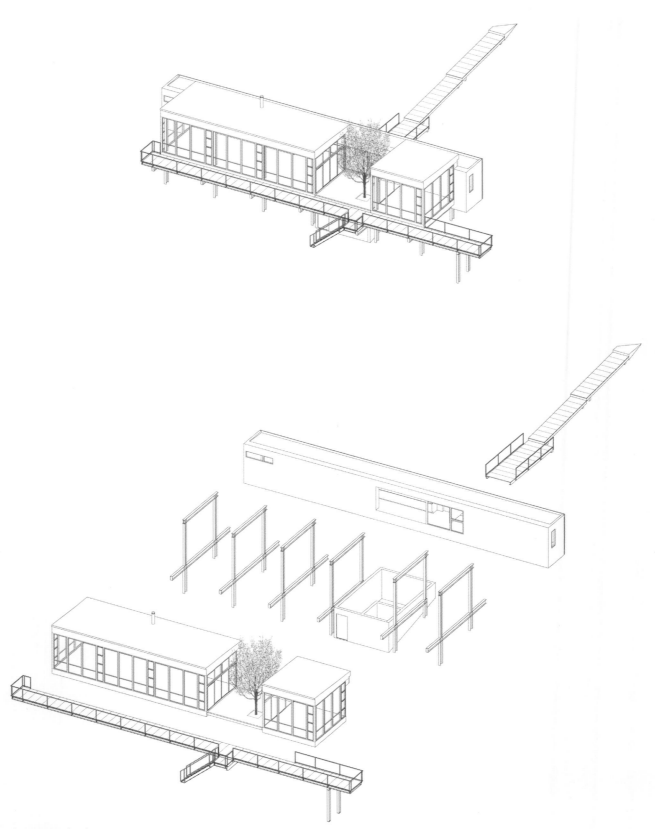

Axonometric view

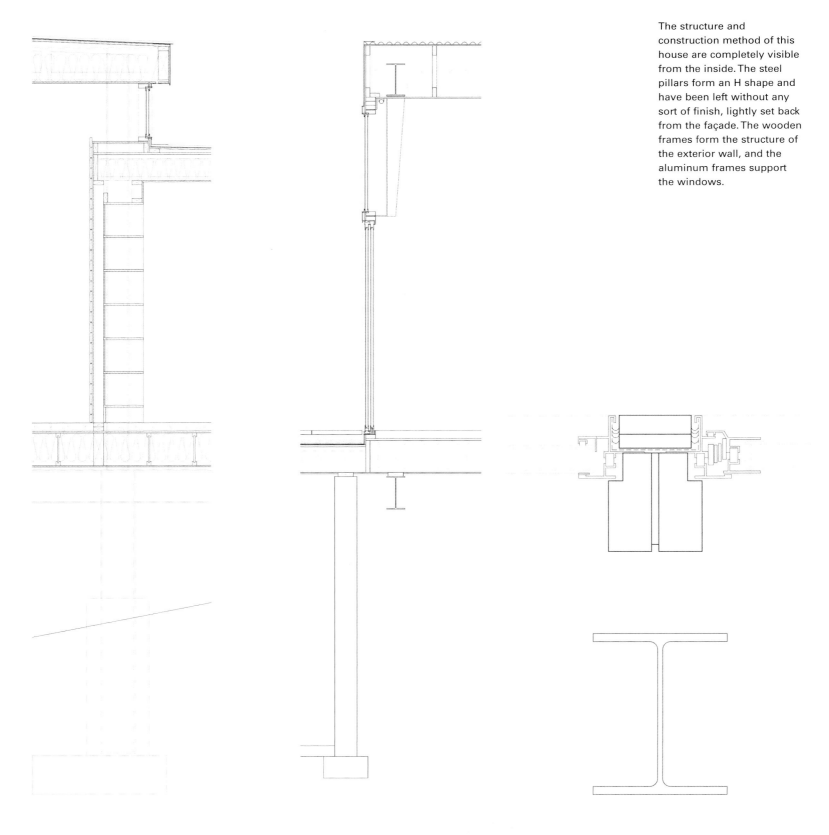

The structure and construction method of this house are completely visible from the inside. The steel pillars form an H shape and have been left without any sort of finish, lightly set back from the façade. The wooden frames form the structure of the exterior wall, and the aluminum frames support the windows.

Construction details

The glass covering, far from offering large openings to the outside, acts as ideal insulation against the area's climates, provides views of the internal structure of the house, and, through the reflections in the brown glass, integrates the house with the environment.

NIGG HOUSE

Architects: **GRASER ARCHITEKTEN**

Location: BIEL, SWITZERLAND

Date of construction: 2001

Photography: ©THOMAS JANTSCHER (EXTERIOR),

LILI KEHL (INTERIOR)

For a long time the area of land where this house stands was categorized as non-developable. When the administration lifted the restriction, the excessive construction that followed became typical in the area. Houses were built one next to the other, with no views and little privacy. The challenge of this project was to use the 5810 square foot plot to create a spacious house, that would maximize the amount of natural light and protected the privacy of its occupants. The house also had to be adapted for people with disabilities.

The composition is based around three volumes that revolve around a central patio, which all the rooms of the house face, thereby solving the problem of privacy. To take advantage of the uneven plot, according to the character and privacy required in each space, a volume was positioned at the higher part for the living areas, with direct access to the outside, and another was suspended on piles that houses the bedrooms. The lowest part of the plot, beneath this volume, was used for the main entrance and the garage. A third longitudinal volume on one side of the composition houses the circulation, taking the form of a gentle ramp, which connects all the spaces.

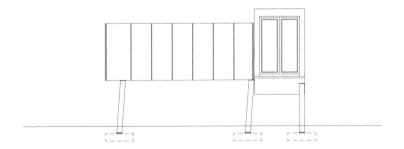

The three volumes that
compose the house act as a
self-supporting structure, the
floor, walls, and ceiling
creating a single shell. The
internal walls have no
structural function and simply
act as dividing panels.

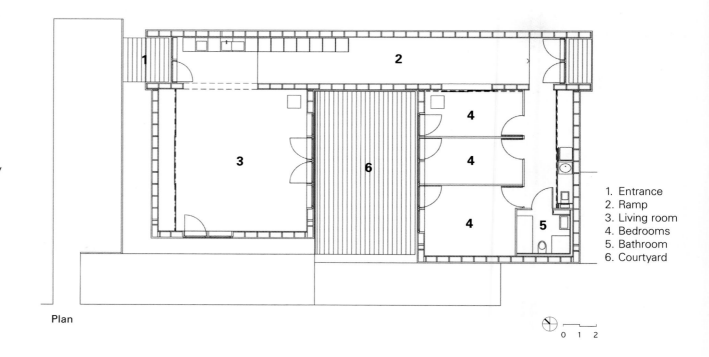

Plan

1. Entrance
2. Ramp
3. Living room
4. Bedrooms
5. Bathroom
6. Courtyard

0 1 2

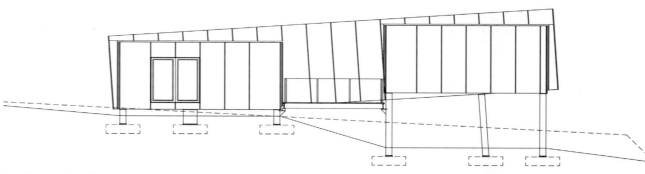

Southwest elevation

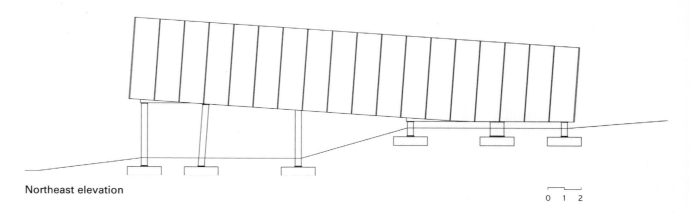

Northeast elevation

0 1 2

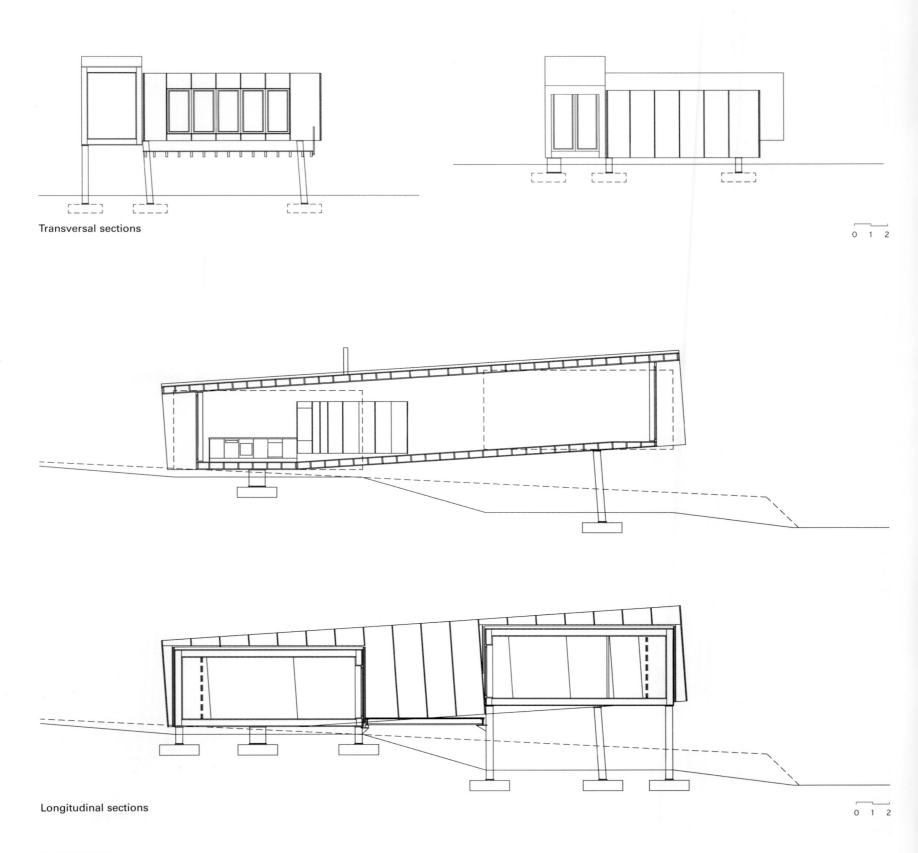

Transversal sections

0 1 2

Longitudinal sections

0 1 2

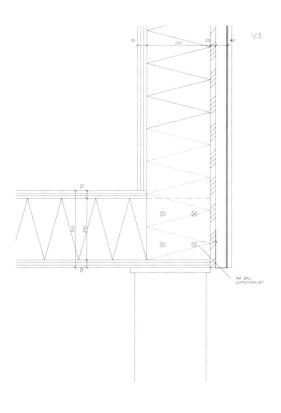

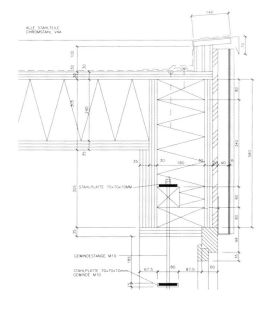

The façades of this house are made from a range of materials: a 0.25-in thick layer of tempered glass, an air chamber, the wooden strips where the glass is held, 0.75-in panels of wood, thermal insulation, and, finally, the interior's plywood panel finish.

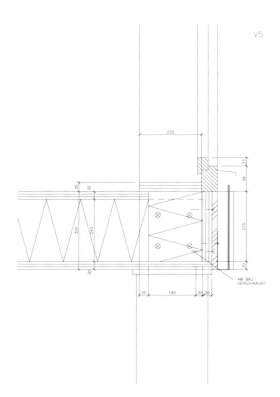

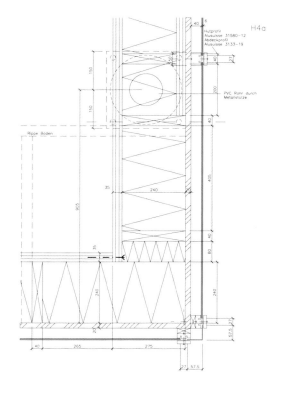

Construction details

To emphasize the idea that the house is buried in the rock and highlight its integration with the environment, the roof has been covered in earth, small rocks, and regional plants.

JENNINGS HOUSE

Architects: **WORKROOM DESIGN**

Location: HOPKINS POINT, VICTORIA, AUSTRALIA

Date of construction: 2002

Photography: ©TREVOR MEIN

Jennings House stands on a 148-acre plot a mere 160 feet from the edge of a cliff overlooking the Indian Ocean in the far south of Australia. The prominent design of the volumes, and its position in the site revolves around the place, the panorama, the wind, and the rocks. The extreme climatic conditions in this part of the country, almost throughout the year, meant the house was to function as a refuge against this extreme environment but at the same time become part of it. The incredible panoramic views, the sounds and the smells of the southern sea, had to be the focal points of the project.

The architects' solution was to create a simple frame on the landscape, an arch oriented to take full advantage of the views and to act as protection for the back yard. That way it became possible to achieve a usable outdoor space for the home. The house is firmly embedded in the landscape via a large opening made in the rock where the house sits. This provides the level of protection the clients needed against the elements and minimized the visual impact the house had on the surroundings.

The long, arched form of the
plan corresponds to the
shape of the mountain where
the house sits and offers the
panoramic views enjoyed
from the house's interior.

1. Courtyard
2. Entrance
3. Garage
4. Storage
5. Bathrooms
6. Master bedroom
7. Dressing room
8. Library
9. Living room
10. Dining room
11. Kitchen
12. Studio
13. Bedroom

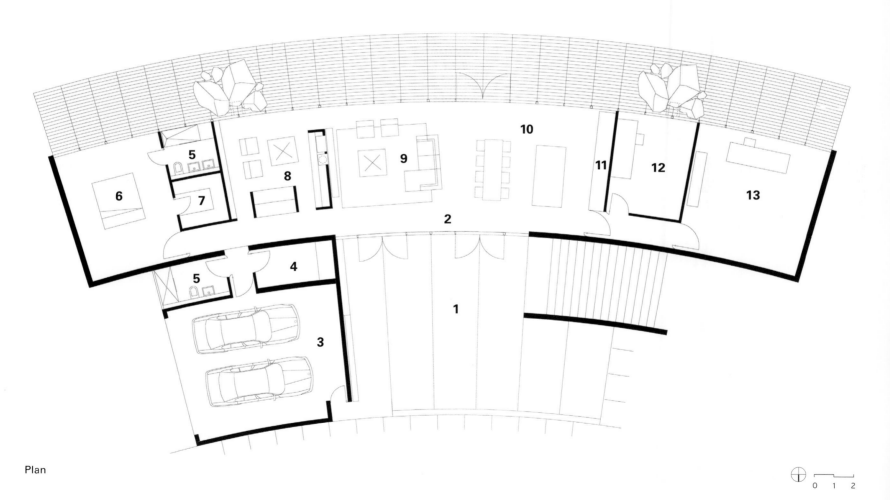

Plan

HARDIES BLUEBOARD WITH DULUX ACRATEX RENDER FINISH

ATLANTIS DRAINAGE CELL

310MM STEEL BEAM REFER TO ENGINEER'S DRAWINGS

HARDIES BLUEBOARD WITH DULUX ACRATEX RENDER FINISH

310MM STEEL BEAM REFER TO ENGINEER'S DRAWINGS

18MM MDF BOX FOR CONCEALED BLIND

10MM SUSPENDED PLASTERBOARD CEILING. PAINT FINISH.

18MM MDF BOX FOR CONCEALED BLIND

10MM SUSPENDED PLASTERBOARD CEILING. PAINT FINISH.

40MM X 90MM X 450 SPLIT FACE CONCRETE BLOCK WALL LINING

140MM REINFORCED CONCRETE BLOCK WALL. REFER TO ENG DETAILS.

100 X 50 MM ST LUCIA GLAZING SUITE NATURAL ANODISED FINISH TO INSIDE SECTION. POWDERCOAT FNISH TO EXTERNAL CLIP

100 X 50 MM ST LUCIA GLAZING SUITE NATURAL ANODISED FINISH TO INSIDE SECTION. POWDERCOAT FINISH TO EXTERNAL CLIP

125MM TH REIFORCED CONCRETE SLAB REFER TO STRUCTURAL ENGINEER'S DRAWINGS.

WATERPROOF MEMBRANE ON SCREED REFER TO STRUCTURAL ENG. DETAILS.

125MM TH REIFORCED CONCRETE SLAB REFER TO STRUCTURAL ENGINEER'S DRAWINGS.

WATERPROOF MEMBRANE ON SCREED REFER TO STRUCTURAL ENG. DETAILS.

In this house the frames of the windows are hidden behind a false plaster ceiling that hangs from the framework of the roof. The lower edges of the windows are inserted into a continuous channel built into the floor's framework.

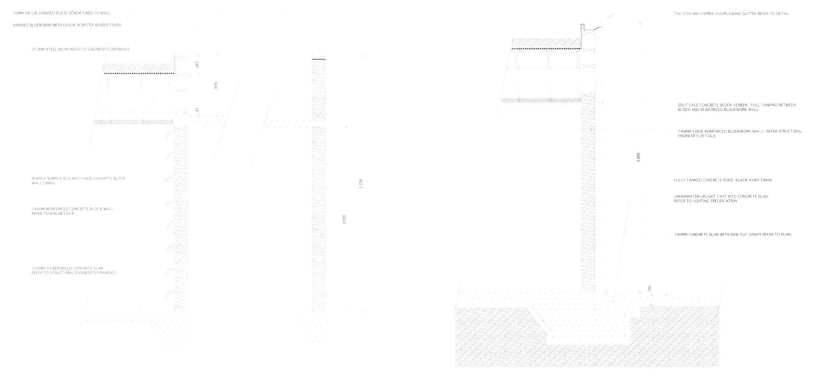

10MM HD GALVANISED PLATE SCREW FIXED TO WALL

HARDIES BLUEBOARD WITH DULUX ACRATEX RENDER FINISH

310MM STEEL BEAM REFER TO ENGINEER'S DRAWINGS

40MM X 90MM X 450 SPLIT FACE CONCRETE BLOCK WALL LINING

140MM REINFORCED CONCRETE BLOCK WALL REFER TO ENG DETAILS.

125MM TH REIFORCED CONCRETE SLAB REFER TO STRUCTURAL ENGINEER'S DRAWINGS.

700 X 90 MM COPPER OVERFLOWING GUTTER REFER TO DETAIL.

SPLIT FACE CONCRETE BLOCK VENEER. FULL TANKING BETWEEN BLOCK AND REINFORCED BLOCKWORK WALL.

140MM THICK REINFORCED BLOCKWORK WALL. REFER STRUCTURAL ENGINEER'S DETAILS.

FULLY TANKED CONCRETE POND. BLACK PAINT FINISH.

UNDERWATER UPLIGHT CAST INTO CONCRETE SLAB. REFER TO LIGHTING SPECIFICATION

100MM CONCRETE SLAB WITH SAW CUT JOINTS REFER TO PLAN

Construction details

The façade's bluntness was achieved thanks to a simple construction method used by the architects, casting the metal profile that supports the window in the concrete slabs. This method aligned the glass with the edges of the slabs and solved the problem of insulating the water.

HOUSE IN RIBEIRÃO PRETO

Architects: **ANGELO BUCCI, FERNANDO DE MELLO FRANCO, MARTA MOREIRA, MILTON BRAGA**

Location: RIBEIRÃO PRETO, SP, BRAZIL

Date of construction: 2001

Photography: © NELSON KON

This house in the suburbs of São Paulo in Brazil was built for a young family and consists of a concrete box that seems to be floating above the ground and can be totally opened to the surrounding garden. The project is an exercise in structure, clarity, and bluntness, reflected in a volume, which is both light and robust. The building rests on four foundation piles set five feet into the rocky ground. The piles support two inverted beams, which reach above the ceiling to support the framework of the roof via metal cables and also hold up the floor, which has no beams.

The natural profile of the garden was totally remodified to create a new garden based on three levels and a path between them running from the street to the inside of the house. The 7-foot high front garden defines the site's parameter and consists of an area leading directly from the living and dining rooms. The 6-foot high back garden consists of a more private outdoor area, reserved for the bedrooms of the house. And the 4-foot central garden acts as an intermediate level on entering the house. It is where the structural and constructive richness of the building can be admired.

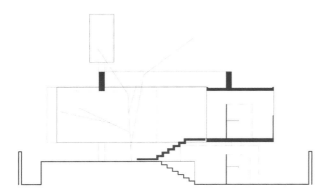

The house is organized around a U, with a central patio, acting as an entrance, that unifies the whole building. The hallway and kitchen are in the central area, just in front of the patio, and the two wings on either side of the hallway are used for living areas and bedrooms.

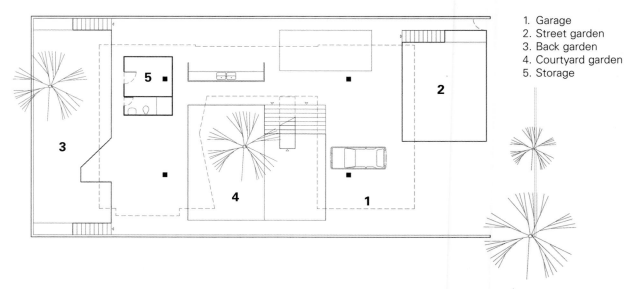

1. Garage
2. Street garden
3. Back garden
4. Courtyard garden
5. Storage

Ground floor

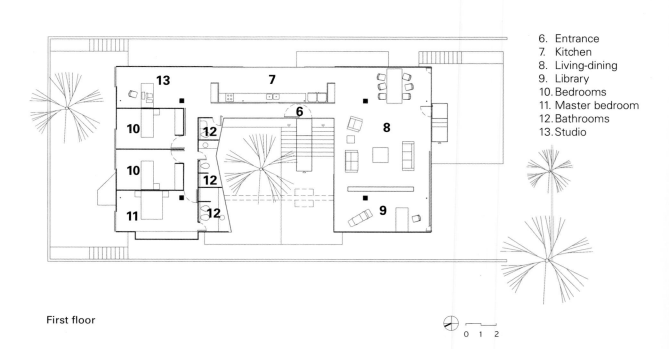

6. Entrance
7. Kitchen
8. Living-dining
9. Library
10. Bedrooms
11. Master bedroom
12. Bathrooms
13. Studio

First floor

0 1 2

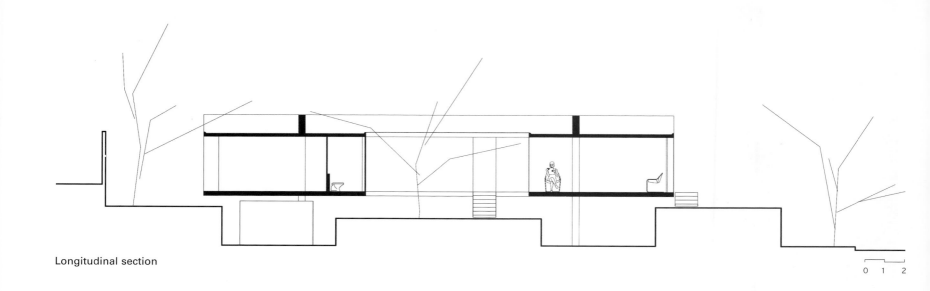

Longitudinal section

0 1 2

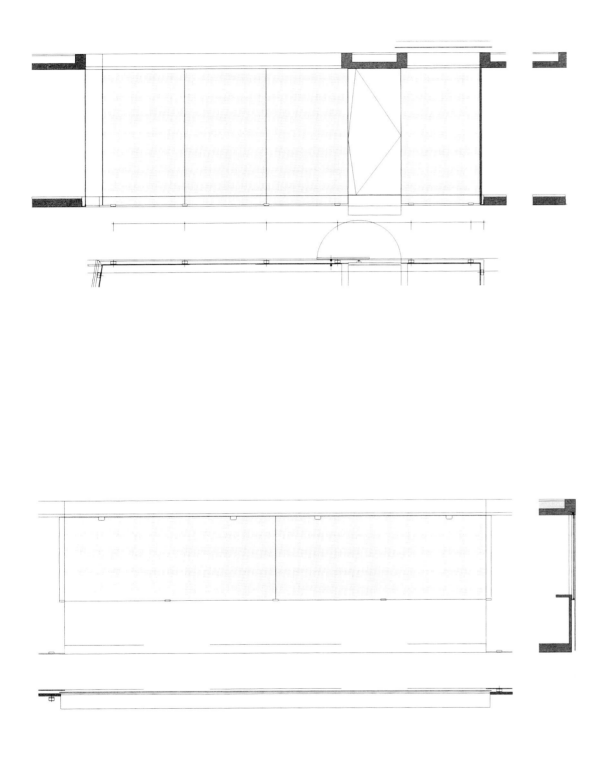

The large glass windows that act as walls for this house can be moved, like sliding doors, allowing the entire house to be open to the outside on days of extreme heat. A double lining of metal on the floor and ceiling framework allows this mechanism to function.

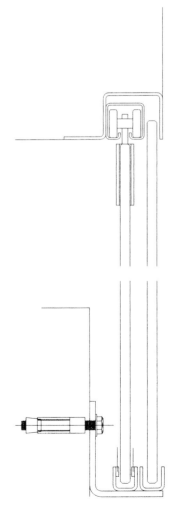

Construction details

The glass in this house, rather than being a decorative element, becomes a structural one, which is essential to the project. The arrangement of the glass sheets, glued to one another and used as walls, is a creative alternative compared to the traditional usage of these materials.

LAMINATA HOUSE

Architects: **KRUUNENBERG VAN DER ERVE ARCHITECTEN**

Collaborators: SAINT-GOBAIN GLASS, VAN RIJN & PARTNERS, RADIX & VEERMAN

Location: LEERDAM, THE NETHERLANDS

Date of construction: 2001

Photography: © LUUK KRAMER

Laminata House redefines the parameters for using glass as a construction material. The material's transparent, slender, and fragile appearance becomes, in this project, translucid, robust, and strong. Despite the application of glass being totally innovative and imaginative, the resulting construction is not merely an experimental prototype; it is a functional building, which satisfies all domestic needs. From the start of the design process, which was based on the premise of using glass as the main construction element, the main aims were to achieve robustness and privacy with this material.

The construction system had to allow for a certain amount of flexibility in the structure to avoid movements of the building that could cause the walls to crack. After a thorough investigation and carrying out various tests it was concluded that the adhesive material of the sheets had to contain silicon to absorb movements of the building itself. Sticking several glass sheets on top of one another attained the strength and resistance of the panels. This system also offers more privacy to the interior as well as allowing natural light to enter.

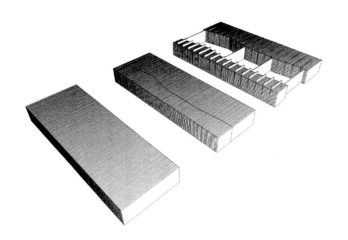

The plan is organized around a central patio, that unifies the building and from where the house can be entered via the garage. The glass sheet walls shut off two bays on both sides of the building; one contains the bedrooms and the other the corridors and a bathroom.

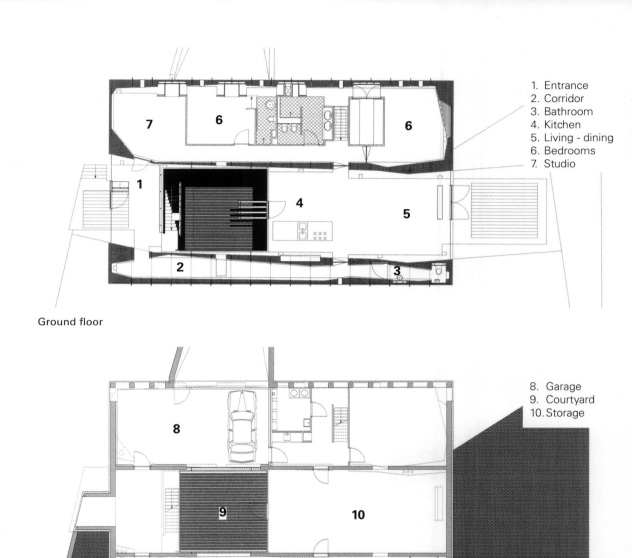

1. Entrance
2. Corridor
3. Bathroom
4. Kitchen
5. Living - dining
6. Bedrooms
7. Studio

Ground floor

8. Garage
9. Courtyard
10. Storage

Basement plan

0 1 2

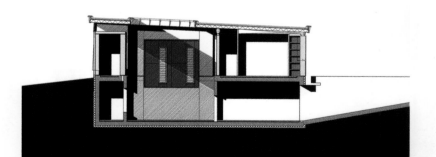

Transversal section

0 1 2

At sunset the metal and glass façade, which opens completely toward the river, looks like an illuminated display case, varying in intensity depending on the activities inside, and giving the passerby a reference point along the river, as if it were some kind of magic lantern.

HOUSE OPPOSITE THE RHINE

Architects: **BMP ARCHITEKTEN**

Location: KOBLENZ, GERMANY

Date of construction: 2002

Photography: © JÖERG HEMPEL

Koblenz is situated where the Rhine and Mosel rivers join in the west of Germany. It is a small city of both historical and architectural importance. The project's design was based on two determining factors, which arise from the features of the plot. It lies just in front of the Rhine River and is surrounded by a collection of classical residential villas. The challenge of this project was to establish a relationship between both the natural and built-up surroundings, while at the same time creating a contemporary house. The project began with a pre-existing two-story building with an attic, whose original structure and volume was conserved. The building's usage, as much for a young family as for offices, determined its formal appearance.

The original roof of the building was destroyed and in its place an extra mezzanine was built as well as a new roof. With this feature they were able to include large terraces, which circle the building giving views of the opposite bank of the river. The front façade was changed completely by the addition of a body of glass that opens in its entirety to the view and makes the inhabitants feel they are just above the river. Concrete, steel, and glass were used for the restoration, which can clearly be seen from the outside.

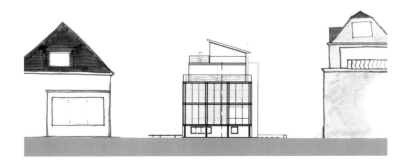

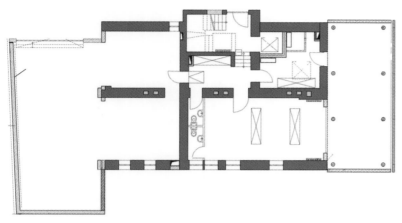

Ground floor

First floor

Second floor

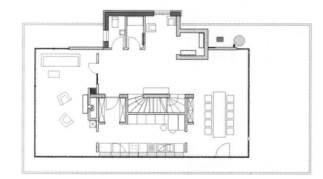

Third floor

0 1 2

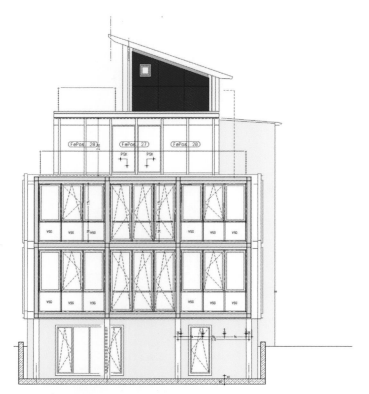

Front elevation

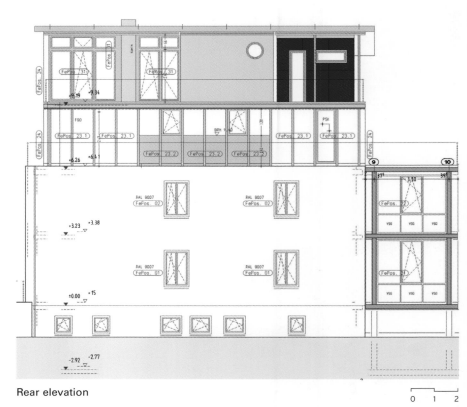

Rear elevation

0 1 2

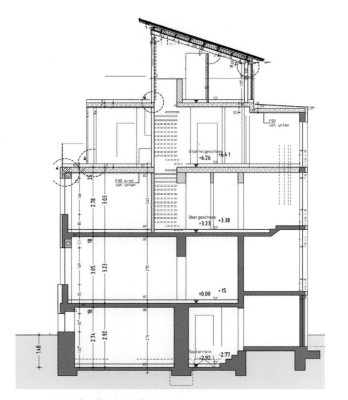

Longitudinal section

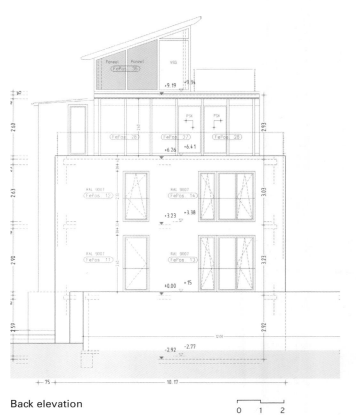

Back elevation

0 1 2

The heavy rainfall and intense cold this area suffers from determined even the smallest details of the façade's finish. This villa has peripheral insulation, present even in the glass doors and windows.

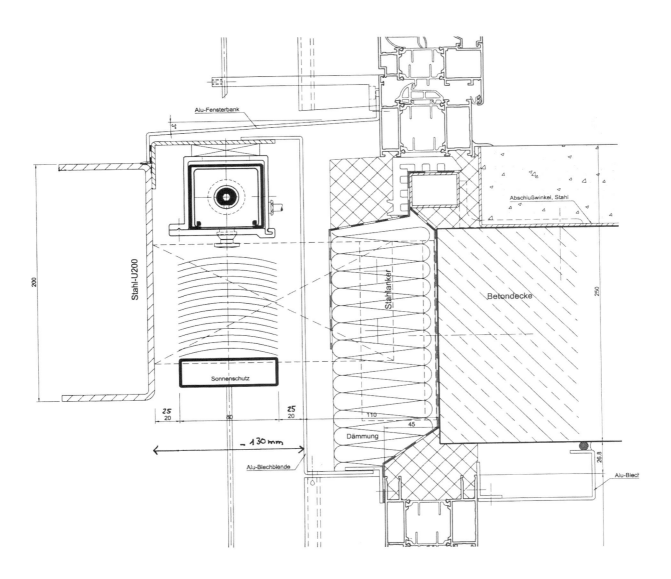

Alu-Fensterbank

Stahl-U200

200

Sonnenschutz

25
20

80

25
20

~ 130 mm

Alu-Blechblende

Dämmung

110

45

Stahlanker

Betondecke

Abschlußwinkel, Stahl

250

26.8

Alu-Blech

Construction details

The large glass body that occupies the center of this house consists of a space between the interior and the exterior, relating directly with the house's private garden, the landscape of the surrounding forest, and the interior of the blocks for winter and summer.

TANGLEFOOT HOUSE

Architect: **CUTLER ANDERSON ARCHITECTS**

Location: PRIEST LAKE, ID, USA

Date of construction: 2001

Photography: © UNDINE PRÖHL

The division into two clearly differentiated sections, one used in winter and the other in summer and both joined by a high body of glass makes this house unique. The design reflects the position of the house, in the middle of a dense forest in front of a lake in Idaho where the seasons have completely different climates. The extreme cold of the winter contrasts with the intense heat and wave of mosquitoes that invade the plot in summer. The glass construction works as well in one season as in the other; in the cold months as a large-scale greenhouse and in the warm months as an area protected from the mosquitoes.

The construction is built on a base of reinforced concrete, which houses the bathroom and toilet and insulates the house from the ground, which has undergone special treatment to make it resemble an existing building. This base raises the rest of the construction, where the home is found, maximizing the natural light and giving panoramic views of the surroundings. The large window that joins the two areas of the house is built with aluminum and wooden frames.

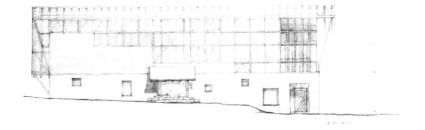

The summer block is smaller
and houses a bedroom with
bathroom and a lounge area.
During the winter this area is
closed off, reducing the surface
area that requires heating.

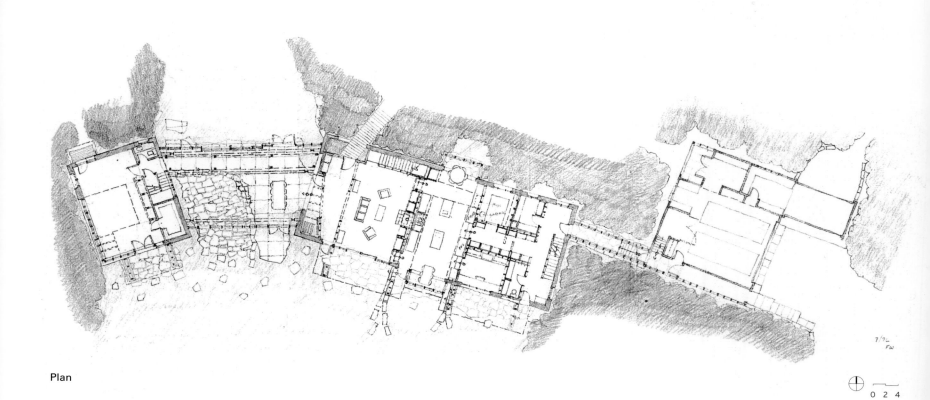

Plan

0 2 4

This gleaming glass box lined with oxidized metal is reminiscent of the region's refined agricultural industrial constructions, and it serves as well as a hi-tech building at the service of its inhabitants.

M-LIDIA HOUSE

Architects: **RCR ARQUITECTES**
Location: GIRONA, SPAIN
Date of construction: 2002
Photography: © EUGENI PONS

The architects defined the initial parameters of this project using three fundamental points: a flat plot with good views, a simple project for a young couple, and a reduced budget. A strategic solution, based on a prefabricated construction, was chosen to complete the project in an effective and profitable way. The entire house was built in the work-shop and basically consists of a box-shape building, with thin walls and windows protected by metal grills. These open outward creating openings that bring the project closer to its environment. This glass box is supported by concrete walls, which form a half-buried enclo-sure containing the garage.

The project uses a symmetrical plan which is closed on the north side, where all the amenities of the house are found, and is completely open to the south, where the communal spaces and bedrooms are found. The two areas generated in the volume are like two small patios and delimit each of the rooms, creating a link between them as well as with the exterior. The positioning of these enclosures make the interior of the house appear as a single space or as three different ones.

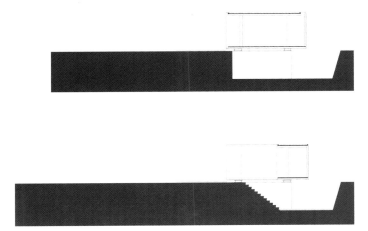

M-Lidia House is located in
Montagut, Girona. Its
implementation on the land
started with the creation of
concrete walls buried in a
small hump to generate
vehicle access to the home.

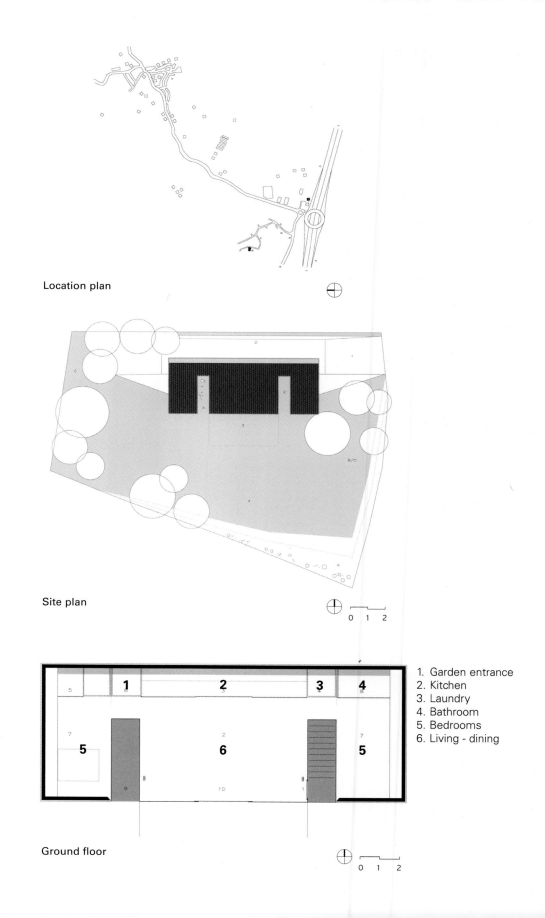

Location plan

Site plan

Ground floor

1. Garden entrance
2. Kitchen
3. Laundry
4. Bathroom
5. Bedrooms
6. Living - dining

The support for the windows in this house comes from the edges of the floor and ceiling framework, freeing the façade of the building from any structural role. The sheets of glass are joined using silicon, giving the building the appearance of a glass box.

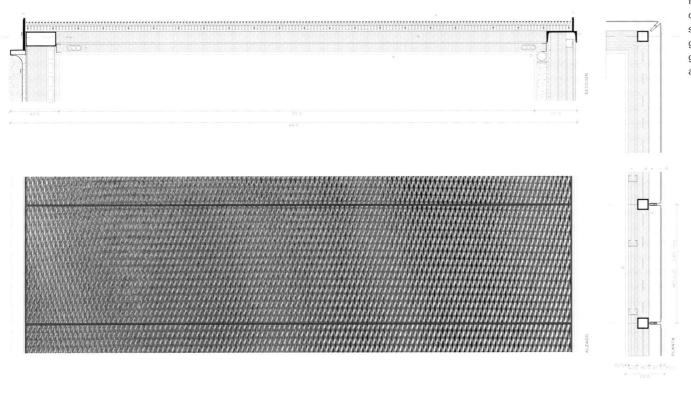

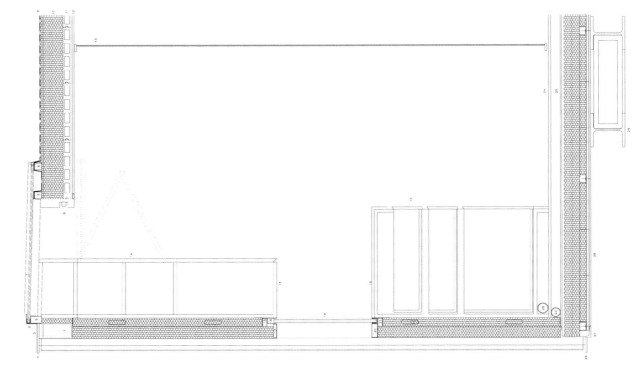

Construction details

The architect's fascination for the innovations of the façades comes from his doctoral thesis, "The Chameleon Skin", on climatic control in architecture using intelligent envelopes, a technological advance regularly applied in different technical applications in architecture.

SENIORVILLA DEYS HOUSE

Architects: **ARCHITECTENBUREAU PAUL DE RUITER**

Location: RHENEN, THE NETHERLANDS

Date of construction: 2002

Photography: © RIEN VAN RIJTHOVEN

A middle-aged couple wanted a house where they could stay until they were elderly. Their aim was to create a wheelchair friendly house, even though at the moment neither use one, without the house appearing equipped for someone with disabilities. An indoor pool was incorporated into the project as the couple wanted to be able to swim everyday, and resistant materials were used so the house would require minimal maintenance. Finally the project would have to integrate harmoniously with the delicate surrounding landscape, on the banks of the Rhine River and near the historic town of Rhenen.

The project responded to all the requirements with a very simple composition based on two single-story rectangular volumes, which run parallel to the Rhine, joined by a third lower central volume, which contains the swimming pool. The longitudinal façades face north and south, taking full advantage of the best panoramic views over the valley and maximizing the contact with the sun. The south façade incorporates a system of aluminum and wooden sheets, which can be folded according to the time of day or the season. This means the level of transparency attained from the large glass surfaces can be easily controlled depending on the climate or the desired amount of privacy.

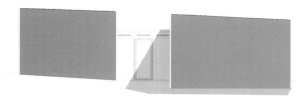

The pool, at the center of the home, unifies the entire piece. Its glass finish allows it to integrate with the other rooms in the house as if it were an interior patio.

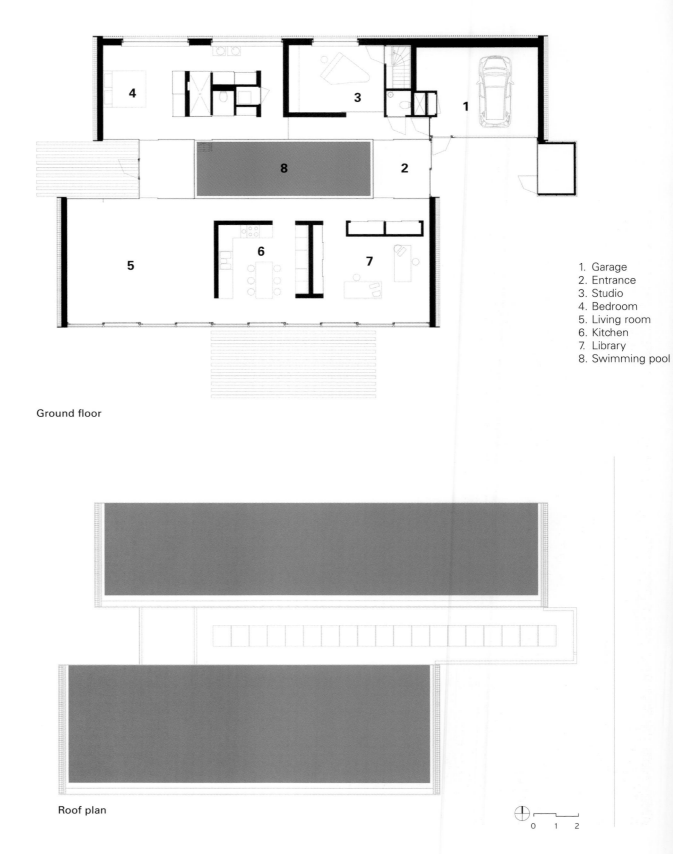

1. Garage
2. Entrance
3. Studio
4. Bedroom
5. Living room
6. Kitchen
7. Library
8. Swimming pool

Ground floor

Roof plan

0   1   2

The roof of the swimming pool is suspended from the roofs of the higher adjacent volumes from metal tension cables, which are subtly hidden behind the glass panels.

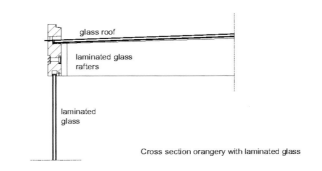

Cross section orangery with laminated glass

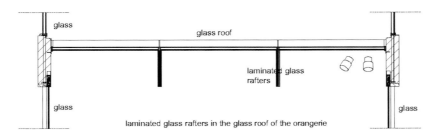

laminated glass rafters in the glass roof of the orangerie

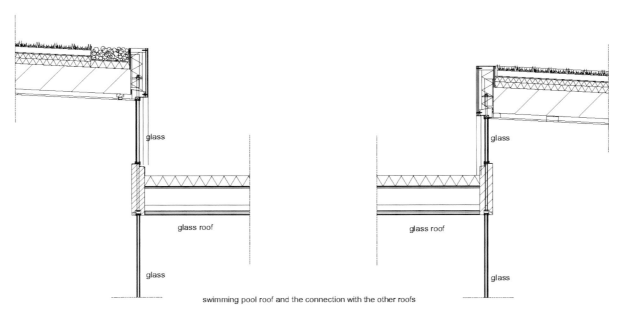

swimming pool roof and the connection with the other roofs

Construction details

The color white is the unifying element between the two different structural systems that compose the house. The metal structure and the large windows open onto the private garden that surrounds the house's living area.

BR HOUSE

Architect: **REINACH / MENDONÇA ARQUITETOS ASSOCIADOS**

Location: BRAGANÇA PAULISTA, SP, BRAZIL

Date of construction: 2004

Photography: © NELSON KON

In this weekend home in the province of São Paulo in Brazil, the architects have drawn on the design premise used in previous projects. The project makes use of various construction techniques, which are applied to different areas of the house depending on their shape and function. A structure of light walls was created for the large living area while for the more intimate areas and those for the amenities a more traditional system of self-supporting walls was used. A large steel rectangle reaching 20 feet in height houses a big living room and a porch, defining the house's meeting and social point. This volume is characterized by its lightness, the collective use of the spaces and the idea of creating a link between the different rooms of the house, and between the house and the garden. The traditional structure of the walls organized in a simple rectangle, however, emphasize the intimacy and seclusion of the bedrooms and bathroom areas.

The house is organized on two levels, which follow the natural slope of the land, and are connected via a corridor and a ramp. This circulation acts as a connecting element between the two different construction techniques. The result is a user friendly, functional building, which is adapted to the topography.

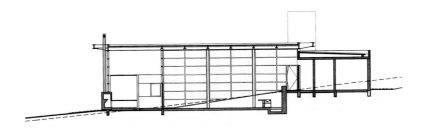

The building has been designed on an L-shaped plan, which contains the private and bathroom areas and surrounds the house's large central space. This is square-shaped and opens completely to the outside.

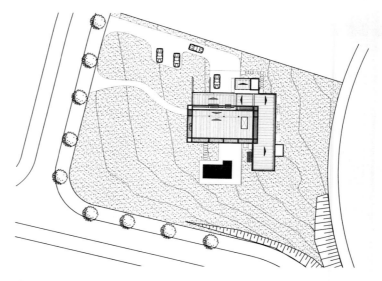

Site plan

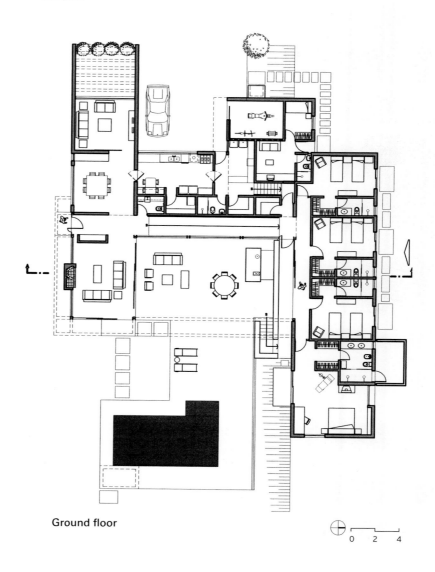

Ground floor

0   2   4

The entrance to the house is on a lower level, which is half-buried and is met by a patio that descends like a natural crack and contains the entrance steps. At the extremes of the building the glass accentuates the folds of the structural walls, which give the composition its form.

CS HOUSE

Architects: **AH& — MIGUEL A. ALONSO DE VAL, RUFINO J. HERNÁNDEZ MINGUILLÓN, MARCOS ESCARTÍN MIGUEL**
Location: SENTMENAT, SPAIN
Date of construction: 2002
Photography: © HISAO SUZUKI

The best virtue of this plot, situated just a few miles outside of Barcelona in Spain, is its elevated position, which provides excellent panoramas. Apart from this the landscape is dotted with residential constructions, and the project had to create a world for the inhabitants away from the strong visual impact of the neighboring buildings. The volume is built from an enclosed structure, which forms the entire building, from the excavated floor to the roof, like a skin that folds to create the different rooms of the house. The folds generate openings, mainly toward the northeast and southeast depending on the views desired and the function of the spaces inside.

The organization inside allows the bedrooms and the living and dining area, which are downstairs, to face the garden, which offers protection from the immediate neighbors thanks to its thick vegetation. In contrast, the first floor needed a uniform, diffused light, and so has a translucid façade facing the opposite direction to the ground floor, and opening to the distant views through large windows at either end of the volume. There is a terrace here that runs around the house and highlights the opening to the sky.

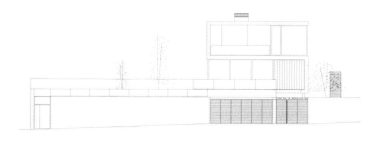

The ground floor, where most of the house is organized, has a longitudinal plan running from south to north. On the east side are all of the amenities, such as the kitchen, bathrooms, and cupboards, while on to the west are the bedrooms and the living area.

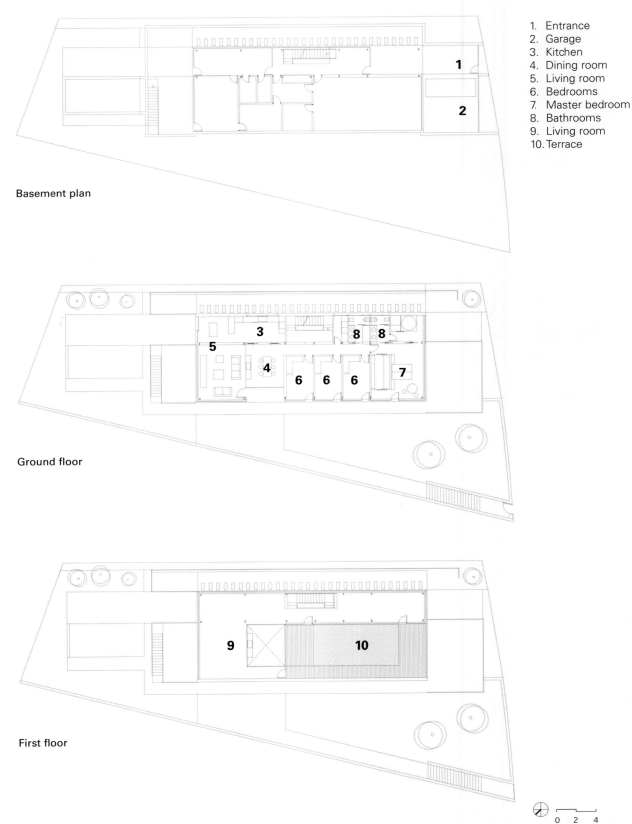

Basement plan

Ground floor

First floor

1. Entrance
2. Garage
3. Kitchen
4. Dining room
5. Living room
6. Bedrooms
7. Master bedroom
8. Bathrooms
9. Living room
10. Terrace

0   2   4

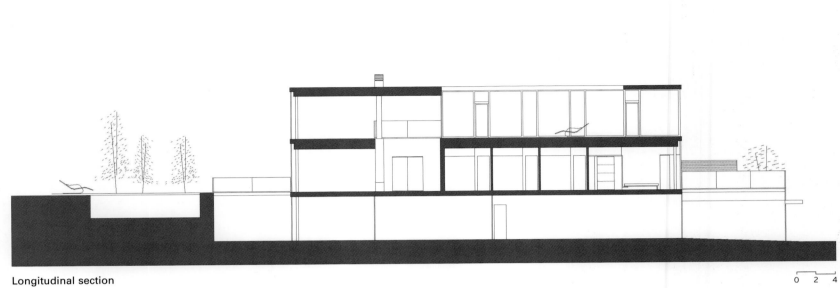

Longitudinal section

0 2 4

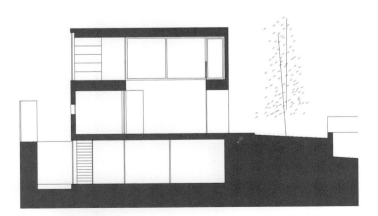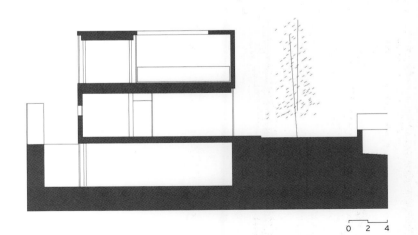

Transversal sections

0 2 4

Possible overheating in the summer is avoided thanks to the natural protection provided by the foliage of the trees, as well as a ventilation system that works in the same way as a chimney. The lack of leaves on the trees in the winter allows the solar radiation to pass and energy to be stored inside the house.

SOLAR TUBE HOUSE

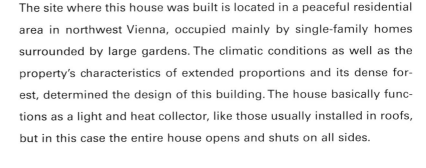

Architects: **DRIENDL ARCHITECTS**

Location: VIENNA, AUSTRIA

Date of construction: 2001

Photography: © BRUNO KLOMFAR, JAMES MORRIS

The site where this house was built is located in a peaceful residential area in northwest Vienna, occupied mainly by single-family homes surrounded by large gardens. The climatic conditions as well as the property's characteristics of extended proportions and its dense forest, determined the design of this building. The house basically functions as a light and heat collector, like those usually installed in roofs, but in this case the entire house opens and shuts on all sides.

The dense forest surrounding the house allowed the use of large glass surfaces on the façades of the house, which overlap and curve to optimize the heat obtained during the colder months of the year. Since so many of the floors and interior elements are made of glass, the center of the house acts as an indoor atrium, connecting the entire composition. Also, the glass covering gives the impression that the surrounding trees define the limits of the interior space. Due to the use of prefabricated units and very basic materials, the construction took only five months, from April to August 2001. This constructive solution saved money, energy, and time.

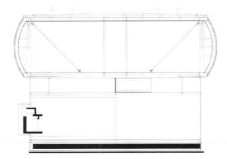

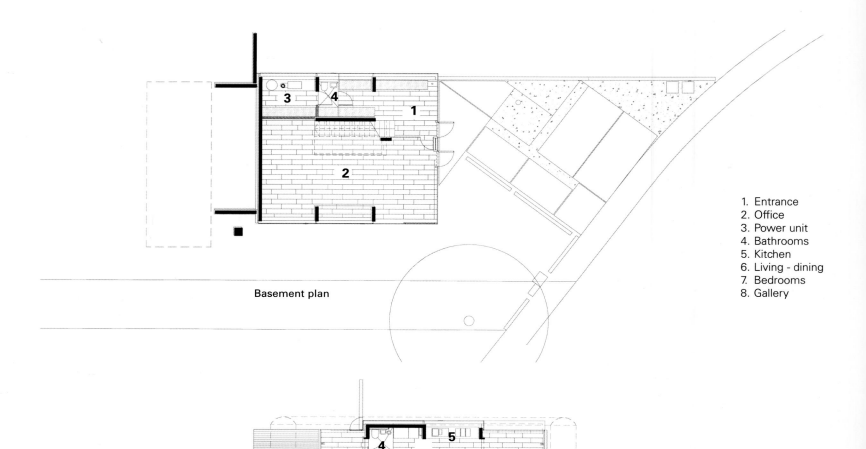

Basement plan

1. Entrance
2. Office
3. Power unit
4. Bathrooms
5. Kitchen
6. Living - dining
7. Bedrooms
8. Gallery

Ground floor

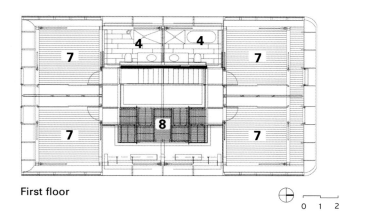

First floor

0 1 2

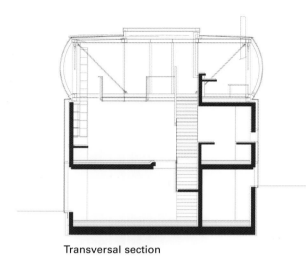

Transversal section

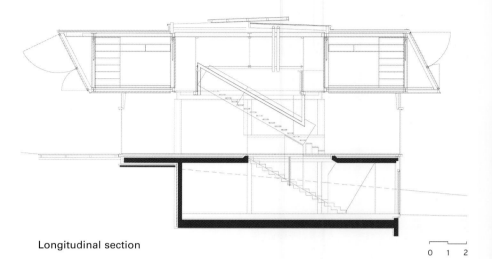

Longitudinal section

0 1 2

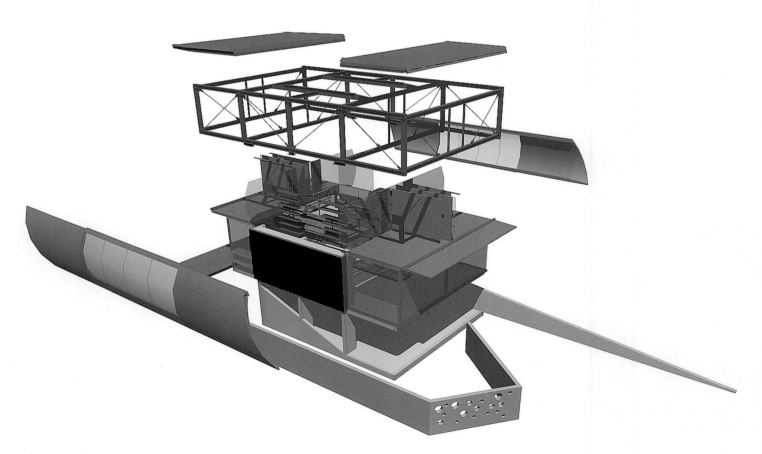

Axonometric view

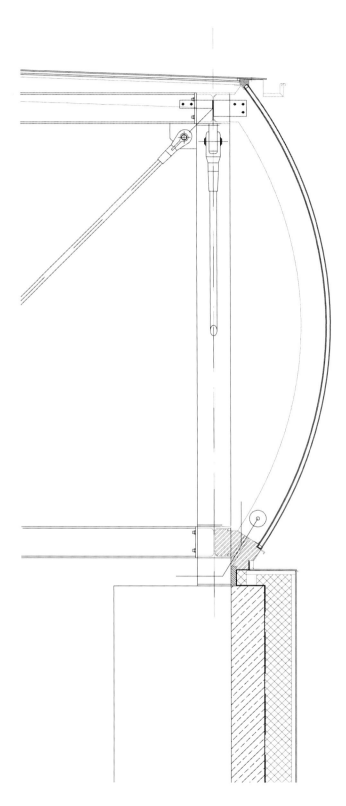

The cross section shows the main materials that compose this house: reinforced concrete, which forms the base structure; the metal framework that gives form to the space; and the prefabricated panels and glass used as covering.

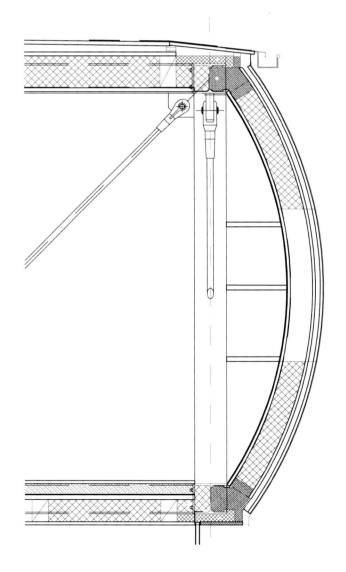

Construction details

The outside of the house is composed of large windows, frames, anodized aluminum mullions, and silver blinds. The proportion and distribution of these elements according to the needs of each room creates an interesting geometrical visual effect from the outside.

ROSZAK HOUSE

Architects: **THOMAS ROSZAK**

Location: CHICAGO, IL, USA

Date of construction: 2002

Photography: © JON MILLAR, HEDRICH BLESSING

This house, in the suburbs of Chicago, is the residency of the architect, his wife, and their three young children. The original idea for this project's design was to come up with a house that fulfilled the needs of a young family but at the same time looked to the future, in terms of its appearance, its functions and the way in which it adapts to the expectations of the family. Aside from the building's physical appearance of concrete, metal, and glass, its modern character comes from the computer system that controls a large part of the functions of the house. A remote control can be used to adjust the heating, program the security system, turn the television on or off, change a CD, open or shut the outside blinds, or control the interior lights.

The design stems from a 16-feet x 16-feet structural module, which functions as an ordering parameter for the building. All the rooms have these measurements with the exception of the living room and the garage which measure 24.3-feet x 32.6-feet. Each module is separated by an intersticial space, which allows each room to be free and spacious. These intersticial spaces house the amenities or circulation elements like corridors, stairs, hallways, pipes or cupboards. The formal and structural clarity is reflected in a transparent design where each room works independently or in conjunction with the others and has a close relation with the outside.

Even the smallest details like tiles,
lights, or windows correspond to
the orthogonal geometry that
regulates the whole building.
The design of the garden, which
is organized along more organic
lines, contrasts with and gives
emphasis to this characteristic.

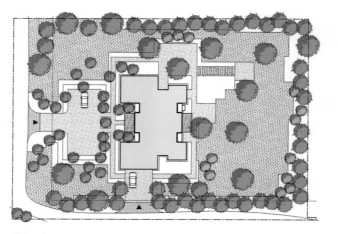

Site plan

1. Entrance
2. Living - dining
3. Kitchen
4. Terrace
5. Exercise room
6. Garage
7. Meditation room
8. Laundry
9. Master bedroom
10. Bathrooms
11. Dressing room
12. Bedrooms
13. Library

Ground floor

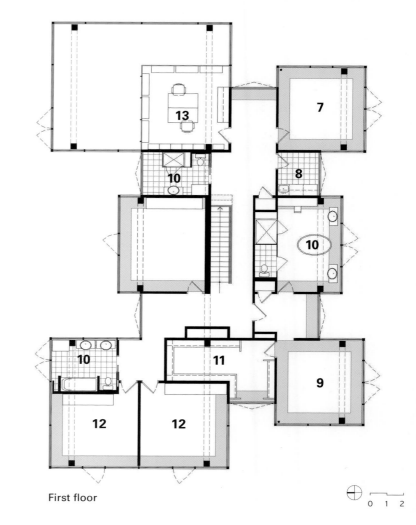

First floor

0 1 2

The exterior finish of the house, from the façades to the roof, consists of glass strips that can be adjusted depending on the need; whether it be for ventilation, climate control or the privacy of the inhabitants.

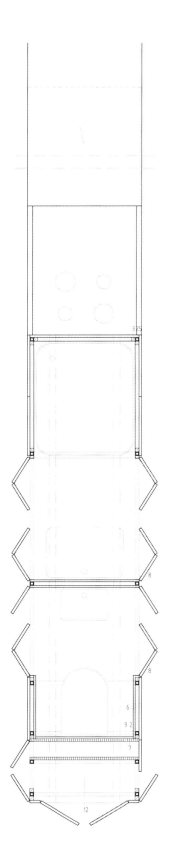

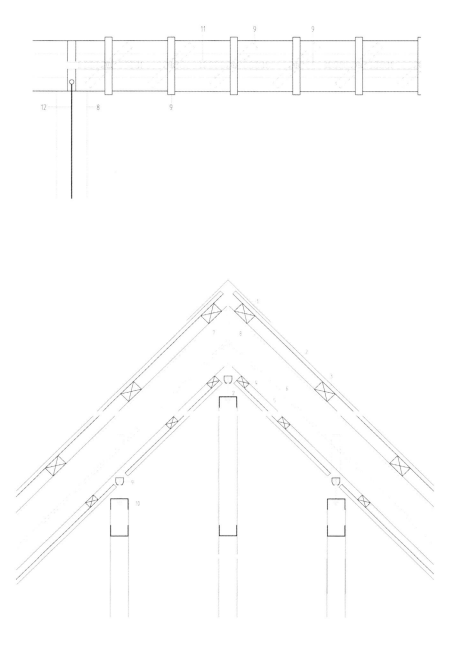

Construction details

Directory

AH& — ALONSO, HERNÁNDEZ & ASOCIADOS
Ciudadela 7, 1°, Pamplona 31001, Spain
T: +34 948 21 17 50
F: +34 948 21 17 91
ah@ahasociados.com
www.ahasociados.com

ANGELO BUCCI
Avenida Faria Lima 1234/121, São Paulo 01451 001, Brazil
T: +55 11 3815 1171
angelobucci@spbr.arq.br
www.spbr.arq.br

ARCHITECTENBUREAU PAUL DE RUITER
Leidsestraat 8-10, Amsterdam 1017, The Netherlands
T: +31 (0)20 626 32 44
F: +31 (0)20 623 70 02
info@paulderuiter.nl
www.paulderuiter.nl

BMP ARCHITEKTEN
Süchtelner Straße 42a, Mönchengladbach 41066, Germany
T: +49 (0) 2161.248878-0
F: +49 (0) 2161.248878-1
mehring@architekten-bmp.de
www.architekten-bmp.de

CUTLER ANDERSON ARCHITECTS
135 Parfitt Way SW, Bainbridge Island, WA 98110, USA
T: +1 206 842 4710
F: +1 206 842 4420
vanderson@cutler-anderson.com
www.cutler-anderson.com

DETHIER & ASSOCIÉS
Rue Fabry 42, Liège 4000, Belgium
T: +32 (0)4 254 48 50
F: +32 (0)4 254 48 51
architectes@dethier.be
www.dethier.be

DRIENDL ARCHITECTS
Mariahilferstraße 9, Vienna 1060, Austria
T: +43 (0)1 585 1868
F: +43 (0)1 585 1869
architekt@driendl.at
www.driendl.at

FELIPE ASSADI
Málaga 940, Las Condes, Santiago, Chile
T: +56 2 263 5738
info@assadi.cl
www.felipeassadi.com

FEYFERLIK / FRITZER
Glacisstraße 7, Graz 8010, Austria
T: +43 316 34 76 56
F: +43 316 38 60 29
feyferlik@inode.at
fritzer@inode.cc

GRASER ARCHITEKTEN
Neugasse 6, Zürich 8005, Switzerland
T: +41 4 33 66 99 00
F: +41 4 33 66 99 01
architekten@graser.ch
www.graser.ch